KU-310-486

'These thoughts are excellent. Rhidian understands the remit of 'Thought for the Day' perfectly and can make the most familiar truths arresting to non-believer and believe alike. They read as well as they sound.'
The Rt Revd Richard Harries FRSL, author and broadcaster

'Whether considering the morality of praying for Beckham's metatarsal, Middle East peace prospects or the similarities between religion and cricket (both can be "hard to appreciate, tedious and require only our nominal attention") Rhidian Brook's Thoughts are always compelling and often funny too. God is lucky to have him on side.'
Miranda France, author

'Rhidian Brook has made his name as one of the most thought-provoking contributors to the 'Thought for the Day' slot on BBC Radio 4's *Today* programme. In just two minutes and 45 seconds he regularly offers an oasis of calm and reflection in the often bleak landscape of news. So it is an absolute treat to find twenty years' worth of Rhidian Brook's Thoughts in one compendium. Read years later, Brook's clear-sighted observations on contemporary events still pack the same spiritual punch as when he delivered them on the radio. His Thoughts make the point forcefully that while politicians come and go, God doesn't and can be found at the heart of what we do every day, all day – if only we are willing to look for him.'
Christopher Hope, Assistant Editor and Chief Political Correspondent, The Daily Telegraph

'Wise and thoughtful, Rhidian's insightful collection of short-reads is sure to satisfy those seeking more to life – as well as a few who aren't.'
Liz Earle, author, broadcaster and entrepreneur

'Rhidian's Thoughts have kept me rooted to the spot more times than I care to admit. I will give this wonderful book to communicators to show them how to do it, to friends to fortify them, to the lazy to challenge them and to the busy to remind them of things more important.'
The Revd David Stroud, Senior Minister, Christ Church, London

'I know how hard it can be to write 'Thought for the Day'. But as a listener, if I'm not captivated in the first few seconds, it becomes a verbal blur. Not so with Rhidian, whose Thoughts are elegantly crafted with imaginative storytelling and real depth. I always listen and learn. He is one of my favourites.'
Mona Siddiqui OBE FRSE FRSA, Professor of Islamic and Inter-religious Studies, University of Edinburgh

'Thoughts that made me Think. Thoughts that make you think. I asked Rhidian to let me do 'Thought for the Day', but he said no!'
Garry Richardson, Today *programme sports presenter*

'A startlingly profound miscellany of insights into the magic and messiness of everyday life from one of our wisest spiritual and cultural commentators. God be thanked for Rhidian Brook.'
Dr James Orr, University Lecturer in Philosophy of Religion, Faculty of Divinity, University of Cambridge

'Rhidian's determination to find the ineffable in the quotidian is heroic. These gem-like Thoughts sparkle across the diverse territories he traverses, honouring the sacred in the seemingly banal, while challenging societal ills that have gained an all-too-distressing momentum over the last twenty years. And while remaining so well-mannered and jovial too. A triumph!'
Omid Djalili, comedian, actor and producer

Godbothering

Thoughts
2000-2020

Rhidian Brook

spck

First published in Great Britain in 2020

Society for Promoting Christian Knowledge
36 Causton Street
London SW1P 4ST
www.spck.org.uk

Copyright © Rhidian Brook 2020

All rights reserved. No part of this book may be reproduced or transmitted in any form or
by any means, electronic or mechanical, including photocopying, recording, or by any
information storage and retrieval system, without permission in writing from the publisher.

SPCK does not necessarily endorse the individual views contained in its publications.

Unless otherwise noted, Scripture quotations are taken from the New Revised Standard
Version of the Bible, Anglicized Edition, copyright © 1989, 1995 by the Division of Christian
Education of the National Council of the Churches of Christ in the USA.
Used by permission. All rights reserved.

British Library Cataloguing-in-Publication Data
A catalogue record for this book is available from the British Library

ISBN 978-0-281-08389-3
eBook ISBN 978-0-281-08388-6

1 3 5 7 9 10 8 6 4 2

Typeset by The Book Guild Ltd, Leicester, UK
First printed in Great Britain by Jellyfish Print Solutions

eBook by The Book Guild Ltd, Leicester, UK
Produced on paper from sustainable forests

For the bothered

'Religion is human behaviour
Grace is the love of God.'
Marilynne Robinson (From '*Home*')

Contents

Acknowledgements

Thanks to:

Karen Duffy, who suggested my name to the BBC when they were looking for someone to do a *Lent Talk*: "Try Rhidian: he actually believes this stuff."

The producers of 'Thought for the Day' at BBC Religion – David Coomes, Amanda Hancox, Dan Tierney, Rosie Dawson, Phil Pegum, Rosemary Grundy and Christine Morgan – for your unseen and unsung work in helping finesse and caress these Thoughts into something 'hearable'.

Christine Morgan, Head of BBC Religion at Radio 4. Midwife to a thousand Thoughts, including many of these. A more dedicated, skilful, vigilant and wise overseer could not be found in all the airwaves.

My fellow Thoughters. Limitations of space mean I can't name you all here but, collegiately, a special thank you for being brave, grappling this strange and slippery form, and for doing your best to put your truths out there.

The presenters of *Today* for making me feel welcome.

All the drivers who have picked me up at 6.30am and got me to the studio on time. Thank you for letting me read my Thoughts to you.

My guinea pigs – Steve Matthews, Duncan McCloud, Harry Armfield – for letting me test out early drafts.

Godbothering

Philip Law, my editor at SPCK, for thinking there might be a book in all this.

My wife, Nicola, who helped me find the meaning.

The Still Small Voice.

xii

Introduction

You've got a day. To write 500 words. About something in the news. Through the prism of your faith. But don't preach. You must not say anything that might offend. Make sure the words contain enough theology to satisfy the remit. Stay true to your faith. While remembering that the vast majority of people out there don't share it. There is no 'we' on 'Thought for the Day'. Don't be platitudinous. Be original. Write as though addressing one person. But deliver them to six million. You'll be live on Radio 4. In the middle of the most influential political news programme in the country. Read it in under three minutes. Ideally, two minutes and 45 seconds. Be ready for feedback. Expect criticism. Maybe even hostility. You'll get paid £90 pounds a pop. Don't give up the day job.

In 1999, I was asked to try a run of thoughts on Radio 4's 'Thought For The Day'. Back then, I knew it as 'a spiritual talk,' given by a rabbi or a bishop, that went out just before 8am on the *Today* programme. I'd heard it referred to (affectionately and pejoratively) as the God-slot, but I'd never considered what it was doing there or who, other than professional religious leaders, got to do it. Its meditative tone seemed anomalous in such a punchy, political show. Yet I was not a devout *Today* listener and wasn't yet aware of Thought's significant place in the nation's consciousness. I accepted the invitation and, a few weeks later, a letter with guidelines (roughly as per above) came in the post. I had my trial run of three in April 2000 in the safer Saturday morning slot and, despite my earnest, dry-mouthed efforts, was later told I'd passed the audition. Twenty years and 200 or so broadcasts later, I find myself still on the rota and in the privileged, if increasingly threatened, position of doing 'Thought For The Day'.

They're a challenge to write. It takes a lot of thought, a little guile, some poetry and – Lord, help! – some inspiration. I've written advertising copy, articles, short stories, novels, film and TV scripts, but Thought is a form *suis generis*. Part mini-meditation, part mini-essay, part something I can't quite define (see the poem below for an attempt). Every Thought requires a script and every script has to be written, rewritten and then checked by a producer at the BBC, the day before broadcast. What you write is subject to the contingency of events and the day you've been allotted. It is written to be read out loud (I choose words for sound as well as meaning); sentences have to roll, syntax has to sooth but then snap; paragraphs have to fit together. It's a tough little construction.

If the form is tricky, the greater challenge is the content. How to see God in the quotidian, describe the ineffable in the unfolding news stories of the day and make these connections for people half listening, half caring or fully annoyed! I know just how irritating 'Thought For The Day' can be to some listeners (they write: 'Dear Mr Brook, I wish you would stop ruining my mornings banging on about your special friend…'). There are the people who have a settled belief that there is no God and that all religion is bogus. Then there are the religious for whom no one is ever religious enough. And then there is a third group – a bigger group in my mind – of people who are not sure, a bit weary, a bit wary and burdened with the troubles of the day ahead. It's this last group I keep forefront of mind when writing. I try to put myself in the shoes or slippers of a morning listener who has other things on their mind and whose tolerance levels go off like a Geiger counter upon hearing the name of Jesus.

A 'Thought for the Day' is an opportunity – a privileged space – to plant one helpful thought in the listener's or reader's mind. Something that gets them thinking. Something that might even lift that burden. It may well trigger ridicule, occasional outrage or stone-cold indifference. Yet, if anything, this makes you work at the words a little harder. In the end, Christianity is a faith built on a God proclaimed as The Word; anyone who wants to proclaim this should choose and use their words carefully.

I have not always believed in this God. When I came to faith – dramatically in my late twenties (another story) – I went from being someone who was lazily agnostic to someone who saw God as ultimate reality, a God intimately involved with humanity. I had a powerful desire to talk and write about this. I became one of those people I'd once mocked: one of those 'Godbotherers'; someone who bangs on about this God, even when uninvited. Of course, it's a derogatory term, but it contains another meaning. Namely, that there is a God worth bothering about; a God who is – whether we are bothered about Him or not – bothered about us. That there is a God who is bothered is a piece of news worthy of a slot in any programme; worth saying to one person or six million.

Rhidian Brook
October 2019

Thought poem

In 2015, I wrote this Thought poem for National Poetry Day. In it, I attempt to describe what I think 'Thought For The Day' tries to be, and what it is.

It's time for Thought
And there's two minutes-forty
To put some glory
In the morning's story,
To make something meaningful
Of what is topical.
To see the spiritual
In all this material.
Time to get the words right
To set the world straight
To give a different take
And shed a different light
To kick against the pricks
Of the daily grind.
To grab a truth worth hearing
To have a quiet word
Amidst the cut and thrust
Of opinion and cross-question.
To offer reflections
From Faith's deep wisdoms
To speak for and against the absurd
To admit the world-sorrow
But not let it have the final word.

It's slipped between
What The Papers Say
And that taped section which
(On any given day)

Thought poem

Reports a sparrow's falling
A kingdom dividing;
And the weather
(Bad and changing).
This daily anomaly
Can't be sermon
And not quite homily,
Preach and be damned
But sound right about what's wrong.
Mine for the good
In the ore of the bad
For a single pearl make a dive
Say there's a God:
Or hint that there might be
Keep the rumour alive.
But don't get ethereal
Keep things reasonable
Don't peddle consolation
Or the best available illusion
Tell a truth, but tell it slant
If not truth then something equal to it.
Make sense of the din,
The savagery, the wonder and triviality,
If you can.

Think of the listeners
Put yourself in their ears
The invisible throng,
Half listening, heckling,
Shaving, commuting.
You're background noise,
To all this thrum
A still, small voice vying

Godbothering

With all the striving.
Truth and platitude sound alike to someone not listening.
The world is dying
To hear something better,
But at this time of morning
It's hard to catch
Other ways of seeing and being
Of doing and living
When you need
To get going,
And a bigger story's breaking
And stocks are tumbling
Empires are crumbling
And they're announcing
The fall
Of kings and companies
The start of wars
And the whole world's ending.

The clock is ticking
Everything atrophies
And things fall apart.
Dare you say
There's something lasting?
You have mere moments
To risk the invisible
Back the un-provable
Stake all on the intangible.
Be still, and know
There's a place
A three-minute space
(The time it takes to boil an egg)
To hear a different voice, another noise

Thought poem

Clear your throat (Yes, it's live)
Speak of more
Than what we simply see and hear,
The something, not the nothing.
No need to start a creed, or lay a law
Say what you think this life is for.
Give some grist,
Blow a breeze, throw a seed
From your studio chair,
From this Kingdom of the air.
Announce good news is near
Before we're off and on our way
And whatever you do, whatever you say
Make it a Thought
That lasts a day.

8.10.2015

Jesus on the Stock Exchange

I once had a job as a telephone salesman. On my first day, the company gave me a sales script that said that if I was having trouble persuading the client to invest their money, I should try using the phrase: 'you have to speculate to accumulate.' I used that phrase with great frequency and confidence. It not only rhymed, but it had an authority about it; it almost sounded like the saying of a wise man.

This week, as people watched the money they had invested in the stock market disappear, many must have wondered if their speculation had been worth it. While dealers told their clients not to panic, to have faith that things would come good in a few days, people must have thought twice about ever investing again. Happily, Monday didn't turn out to be as black as predicted; in fact it only took three days for the mood of investors to pass from despair to a more realistic hope.

Tomorrow it's Good Friday and people will be reflecting on another kind of loss, and hoping for a different kind of return. Like the stock market, faith involves risk. It requires certain investments for which there seems little to gain. For the disciples who had invested so much in Jesus, Good Friday would have been the blackest day of all. With Jesus crucified, what possible return could they hope for?

If faith were a company it wouldn't be listed on the FTSE 100, or found in blue chip portfolios. It would seem both too high risk and too long term. Even riskier than a dot com company. Yet heaven's stock market operates on a different timescale and trades in different commodities. It's made up of seemingly unprofitable investments such as loving your neighbour, giving money away, feeding the poor and the hope of eternal life. If Jesus were to enter the stock market tomorrow, he might well advise dealers to speculate, but not necessarily on the commodities they'd think.

Imagine the scene: electronic boards flashing the day's gains and losses; dealers beginning to trade; a room full of energy and purpose; Jesus walks on to the trading floor; he seems more interested in the actions of the dealers than in the flickering numbers and indexes on the boards. For a while everyone's too busy to notice him; eventually a dealer asks him what he wants. Jesus says, 'I have some investment advice. A share tip if you like: invest in me, invest everything you have and advise your clients to do the same.' The dealer looks at him as if he's mad. 'You must be joking. Where's the profit in that? What would the return be on my investment?' Jesus replies: 'Give me three days and you'll have your answer.'

12.4.2000

—

A good man goes to jail

Sooner or later a good man is going to get into trouble in the world. For his words and actions will eventually bring him into conflict with evil. A year has passed since the 27-year old Englishman, James Maudsley, was arrested by the Burmese government and sentenced to 17 years in prison for protesting against its military junta, a regime that's meant to be responsible for 30,000 murders and the systematic destruction of the Karen People.

Maudsley had already been arrested, imprisoned and tortured for speaking out against the regime just a year before that, only to be deported to England after 99 days in jail on the condition that he would not return illegally. Remarkably this experience did not stop him going back. He got on a plane and went to Burma, where, as he expected, he was arrested and sentenced. He hoped that his arrest would gain sufficient attention from the world's media to bring international pressure to bear on Burma's genocidal regime.

Some might feel that such an action is a waste of a life. Perhaps even selfish or irresponsible. What can one person achieve against a dictatorship? Wouldn't it be better spending 17 years campaigning against the regime rather than being stuck in prison unable to speak?

In a world where people feel overwhelmed by thousands of good causes and unable to do much about any of them, will anyone care about this one?

The Burmese government would surely encourage this line of thinking. They would like us to think him an idealist who got out of his depth and eventually want us to forget all about James Maudsley and his futile gesture. For now they must feel they have succeeded in rendering him ineffective. Alone, cut off from the world, what can this young man do to them now?

As with so many dictatorships in history, this one fails to understand the quiet power of self-sacrifice. The hope-giving act of laying your life on the line for a brother, whatever race, creed or culture. Maybe it takes an idealistic young man to risk his life in such a way. With ideals like these, who can oppose his action, or doubt its ability to change men and knock down empires? James Maudsley's sacrifice is, like any sacrifice, an act of faith, in this case faith in the God who showed us that dying to ourselves brings life to others.

The gospel tells us that the only way to overcome evil is with good. James Maudsley could have sat at home weighing up the pros and cons of going back to Burma. In the end, he found himself compelled by an unstoppable belief in what is right. No evil on earth can resist that.

17.4.2001

—

Break it like Beckham

So, can you remember where you were when you heard the news that David Beckham had broken the second metatarsal in his left foot? I can. I'll never forget it. I was standing in my sitting room late on Wednesday night, checking the news on Ceefax, when I saw the words 'Beckham breaks bone in foot' flashing just above a headline announcing Israel's refusal to withdraw from Palestinian territory. That's a disaster, I thought. That is going to cause pain and anguish to millions of people, and my immediate response was to pray. It was the only thing to do. There was no way this situation could be turned around without supernatural help. I know I should have been praying for the peace of Israel instead of a little bone in a footballer's foot, but I just couldn't help myself. The news seemed, dare I say it, more pressing.

The next day, my inordinate concern for Beckham's foot didn't seem so misplaced. The Prime Minister interrupted a cabinet session to say that Beckham's recovery was of paramount importance to the nation and many of the country's papers were calling for us to pray for Becks. By Friday, *The Sun* newspaper printed a life-sized picture of the England Captain's Left Foot on their front cover and implored its readers to lay hands on the picture and make David better. Which throws up an interesting theological question: if Beckham's foot does get better, will it be down to the father or to *The Sun*?

This all may seem a little out of proportion, but the fact is, more people in this country will be thinking about Beckham than Bethlehem in the next few weeks. We shouldn't be surprised. Football is one of the biggest religions in the world, with a faithful and zealous following. It's home to much superstition and a lot of spontaneous prayer request. I've seen more heavenward imploring at soccer stadiums than I've seen in most churches.

People generally pray – really pray – about things that immediately affect them. Which is a good starting point. Jesus encouraged us to be real in our communication with God, to share what's on our hearts and minds, rather than get all pious about what we should be praying for. What's the point in praying for world peace if we're not able to pray for peace in our own lives, the debts we have, our failing relationships, our sick neighbour? Our prayers don't have to be long and complex. 'Oh God, Please help!' is as real a prayer as any.

God's surely big enough to work out what we're saying, and if we pray enough, maybe he'll give us the grace to pray for things beyond what immediately concern us.

In the meantime, we can surely pray for both Beckham and Bethlehem and hope for the restoration of both. Remember what the word says: How beautiful are the feet of those who bring good news…

13.4.2002

—

God has left the building

If I were to say the word 'church' to you there's a fair chance you'd picture a building. If I were to wander around London asking where I might find God, I'd probably be directed towards a cathedral, or a mosque or synagogue, depending on who I bumped into.

Man's been putting God in buildings for centuries, and there are plenty of buildings all around the world that make special claims for God's residence. Not surprisingly, the buildings become sacred places that man is willing to protect, defend, even kill for. Like the Golden Temple in Amritsar, or the sacred sites in Jerusalem, or the amazing Mesquita in Cordoba, Spain – a beautiful labyrinthine twelfth-century Mosque with a hideous fifteenth-century church built right in the middle of it. It's enough to make you weep. One, that such a beautiful structure can be ruined; and two, that man really believes that God can be evicted from one building and moved into another.

Yesterday the news came that Israel was withdrawing its troops from all Palestinian territories except the Arafat compound at Ramallah, and the Church of the Nativity in Bethlehem. When the troops first surrounded this building a number of news reports suggested that Christians all over the world would be up in arms at this flagrant attack on a sacred site. Were they really? I didn't meet any. Anyway, is someone being shot at in the spot where Jesus was born really more significant than someone being buried alive in the ruins of Jenin, or blown up in a square in Jerusalem? Man's really lost it when he starts valuing real estate over flesh and blood.

In the Old Testament the temple was the place where God's presence (or Shekinah) was said to be found. Yet the tabernacle was sacred because God was there, not because the site itself was to be worshipped. When Jesus entered the temple in Jerusalem and turned over the market stalls, he was angry at what was being done there; but his zeal was for God not for elegant stones and columns.

Jesus went on to say that he'd destroy this temple and raise it again in three days, but he wasn't talking about a building, he was talking about his own body. He was showing us what a real temple is and where the spirit of God resides. If man really could see himself and his neighbour as the possible temple of God's spirit, then would he be so willing to destroy and kill for land, buildings, walls or churches? We need to stop boxing God into little confined, man-made spaces and then claiming that we own the land rights. God left the temple a long time ago to take up residence in a new one: one constructed from people.

20.4.2002

—

Boys A, B, C and D

Who are we going to blame for the death of Damilola Taylor now that Boys A, B, C and D have walked free? The justice system? The police? The education authorities? Racism? A lack of family values? Or is it, as I heard someone mutter yesterday, all down to 'the youth of today?'

If the case of Damilola Taylor hasn't yet found a culprit, it has revealed an unpleasant truth; namely, that we are part of a culture where violence and contempt are everyday realities for a lot of people, *especially* for the young. You don't have to live on an estate in Peckham to encounter it.

A few weeks ago I went to buy a paper from my corner shop here in middle class, suburban West London. As I walked up my street, three teenage children walked past, aggressively swearing and insulting me. After buying my paper I met the same children waiting at the bus stop. 'I'll teach them a little respect,' I said to myself; but as I got close a small voice said: 'How exactly do you intend to achieve that? Are you going to beat it into them?' I was seconds away from taking their bait.

Respect. It's a big word for today's young. A code of acceptance. A buzzword for being part of the gang. The papers reported that during the Damilola trial, Boys A and B sang gangsta rap songs as they entered the courtroom every morning, as if this somehow proved their guilt. What did they expect them to be singing? I might be able to sit at home and laugh at the mock criminality of an Ali G, or admire the lyrical prowess of a So Solid Crew singing about drugs, guns and running flashy cars on the proceeds of crime; but for many children, with few prospects, and often no father around, these are genuine aspirations.

Detective Superintendent Trevor Shepherd, who led the Damilola investigation, said of all four boy suspects in the case that they did not find one father on the scene, and that they (the children) seemed to be setting their own agendas, their own moral boundaries.

The psalmist says that 'as a father has compassion on his children so the Lord has compassion on those who fear him.' The truth is that many fathers do not have compassion for their children. They leave them to their own devices. To fend for themselves. Perhaps that's why God promises to defend the cause of the fatherless. With an estimated 40 per cent of Britain's youth growing up without a father in the home, maybe we should be taking up this cause with Him, before we start putting the full blame on children.

27.4.2002

An audience of one

Today is judgement day. The day we get to see another contestant cast from the house in *Big Brother* – the television programme where ten people are filmed under 24-hour surveillance and do their very best not to get voted from the house. The weekly eviction, where the household and then the television audience decide who is going to go next, is the most compelling part of the programme. Being mercilessly judged by our peers and then by the nation is a position few of us would want to be in.

Despite what many TV programmes claim, a camera locked on someone 24-hours a day doesn't necessarily tell us what that person is really like. If someone put a camera in my house, you might learn that I was untidy, didn't listen to people when they talked to me, was fussy about my coffee, but you wouldn't get the whole picture – thank God. Put a camera in my heart and mind, then you really would have a revealing programme. I guarantee you would evict me on the spot. As Somerset Maugham once said: 'If you could read my mind you'd think me a monster of depravity.'

For all its revealing observations, *Big Brother* is only judging by appearances. We may see people back-stabbing, manipulating, even cheating, but how much of their behaviour is modified for each other and the camera? How much of what they really think and feel remains unseen? To really judge someone fairly, we need to know what's hidden within; but that is something even real life TV can't achieve. So much of what makes a person what they are is unfilmable.

Meanwhile, back in real-life life, some might say we are already undergoing a 24-hour surveillance; a complete and thorough monitoring, where nothing is being overlooked. The Psalmists tells us that God's eyes are everywhere, seeing the evil and the good, that He knows our thoughts, even the secrets of our hearts. Given that we all fall short of perfection, such scrutiny might be terrifying were our lives being judged by an Orwellian state, or even a British television audience.

But maybe we should take heart. When the time comes for us to be evicted from the planet, we aren't going to be judged by an audience of millions, but by an audience of one. One who knows absolutely everything there is to know about us, everything we've said, everything we've done, and everything we've thought. One who insists that mercy will triumph over judgement.

If we could live every 24-hours as though under the gaze of a loving and yet fair judge, rather than the sometimes limited view of a neighbour, friend or boss, think how much better things would be in the house. There might never be a need to evict anyone, or run away from it all when things got too much.

23.10.2002

—

Guns and God

On Christmas Day I had a lunch with a man who believes in Jesus, owns a Bereta semi-automatic handgun, and is fully prepared to use it in the event of someone breaking into his house.

I wasn't so bothered by the gun, which is fully licensed and safely tucked away in a wardrobe five thousand miles away at his home in Philadelphia. He is an American and in America owning a gun is as normal as owning a lawnmower. What threw me was the idea that a committed Christian was, without equivocation, prepared to kill someone in self-defence.

So after thanking God for our turkey, and telling my son to put away his replica Winchester repeater with richochet sound effect, I asked my American friend how he could square his belief in a God of peace and love with using a gun? I pointed him to the gentle and weapon-free approach of Jesus in the gospels; in reply he directed me to a host of fully-armed, locked and loaded Old Testament characters who illustrate that God doesn't necessarily have a problem with the possession of arms or people using them in his name.

Later that afternoon, we sat down to watch *It's a Wonderful Life*, a film that's about what might happen if a good man despairs and gives up when things go badly wrong. Jimmy Stewart plays the good guy, and it's a character not unlike the one he plays in *Destry Rides Again*, which is about a lawman who tries to clean up the town without using his gun. Stuart has a brave try, but ultimately has to shoulder arms. Not even Hollywood could dream up a satisfactory, gun-free resolution.

Besides, peaceable men, disarming violence without the use of weapons, doesn't make for great drama. In movies people want the good guy to win, but they want him to win decisively and stylishly, and preferably using guns. Even the messianic hero in the film *The Matrix* says he needs guns, lots of guns, to get things done.

The trouble is, there are people in real life who believe that weapons get things done, and right now there's a lot of gun talk and smoke. From the streets of London to the deserts of the middle-east, it seems guns are calling the shots. Cleaning up the town. Giving people what they want. The power to control.

The power that's at work in the gospels involves a different kind of weapon. When Jesus turned up, many were disappointed that the potential saviour of the world didn't even have a scabbard, let alone a real sword. How on earth was this man going to deal with the violence that was to come against him? Was he going to use the mighty power he claimed was at his disposal? Surely he'd at least fight back in the name of self-defence? No. Instead he chose the ultimate weapon with which to disarm evil. Himself.

11.1.2003

—

God's favourite movie

I wonder what God's favourite movie might be. Would he go for a biblical epic, or would he find that all a bit too close to home and settle down to nice romantic comedy or even the irreverence of the *Life of Brian* – a film which after all shows how foolish people can be when they get too religious?

God's movie preferences are something Hollywood's having to think about right now. Given the phenomenal success of the *Passion of the Christ* – a film with no studio backing that's enjoyed the second best opening take in history – there's clearly money to be made in the religious market. I guess we can expect a glut of further epics to start appearing on our screens.

In a way, this would be a shame – for spiritual stories don't have to be dressed up in robes, have a soft glow around the edges or go for violent realism to ask the big questions. Why, only last week I saw a religious film called *Lost In Translation*. It was the gentle story of two people alone in a foreign land, looking for depth in the cultural shallows of their lives, and it seemed to show something true – namely that people, whether conscious of it or not – have a need for meaningful connection, with each other and possibly with something beyond themselves.

Maybe the division of the world into the religious and the secular, and the separation of supposed religious questions from what we might call questions of everyday life, is a false one – a kind of category error. This was in evidence this week at the National Gallery's El Greco exhibition and also at the National Theatre, where the Archbishop of Canterbury met with Philip Pullman, author of the *His Dark Materials* trilogy, to discuss the meaning of religion in art and literature. On paper it was a contentious prospect: Pullman, whose book had been damned by some religious commentators for his anti-clerical stance, was going head-to-head with the leader of the Church of England. But fairly soon into the discussion it became clear that both men were interested in the same questions: the ones that great art explores and that we all at some stage have to face, namely what it is to be alive, to suffer, to love and to die. In these days of extreme opinion and defensiveness, it was heart-warming to see these two supposed polar opposites magnetized by a common theme. The Archbishop mentioned that his favourite film was *Babette's Feast*. Another subtle film in which the differences between the religious and the secular are bridged and transformed by the creative generosity of the main character. Without forcing it, this tale shows that all of us, the pious and the worldly, have a yearning for real connection and understanding and that stories or art can help bring about enlightenment and revelation.

There are some who say that if you want to worship then go to church, not the movies or art galleries. Walking around the packed El Greco exhibition, it was hard not to think that something more than just art appreciation was taking place. Were the people just admiring the artist's cinematic skill and unorthodox genius; or were they seeing in those other worldly and yet oddly modern figures bursting from the canvasses, something of the divine breaking into their everyday lives, asking them the big questions?

20.3.2004

—

Let's get drunk

I bought my first alcoholic drink when I was 14. I wore a jacket and tie to look more mature and ordered a rum and coke to try and seem sophisticated. I don't know where I'd got the idea that getting drunk was something worth doing – maybe it was peer pressure – but after a few drinks, I noticed we were all saying things, even doing things, we wouldn't normally do. We were losing our inhibitions. There was a lot of laughing, but when I woke up the next day, it didn't seem so funny. I felt terrible. I consoled myself with the thought that the evening must have been successful because we had drunk so much and because I felt so bad.

This week the Prime Minister warned that binge-drinking was fast becoming the new British disease, and that something needs to be done quickly. I'm not sure that changing the licensing laws, the price of drinks, or banning happy hours will get to the root of the problem. A lot of people binge drink to get out of themselves. The terms we use for getting drunk reflect this intention: we want to get smashed, off our heads. Drinking is a way of escaping our troubles – if only for a few hours. Yet people also drink to have a good time; our brains are wired to seek pleasure and man will fill himself with whatever does the job. The trouble is that, in that process, we so often settle for the shadow; the fleeting pleasure of drunkenness is really a blurred glimpse of the real freedom God intended for us.

The Bible sees wine as a sign of God's blessing and acknowledges that it gladdens life. It also encourages us to drink deeply – not with wine, but with God's Spirit. Curiously the activity of God's Spirit seems to have the same effect on people as alcohol. Which is why so many biblical figures experiencing religious ecstasy were accused of being drunk. Indeed, the word ecstasy means to stand outside yourself, to actually be out of your mind.

Jesus, who must have spent a lot of time in bars, was accused of being a drunk. Just as the apostles who, on being filled with the Holy Spirit on the day of Pentecost, were thought to have had too much wine. When Peter had to explain their behaviour to amazed and outraged onlookers, he quoted the prophet Joel, who said that in the last days God would pour out his spirit on all flesh.

The difference was that this spirit was something new. Yes, it would fill people with joy and boldness; yes it would help them lose their inhibitions, make them laugh and cry and even sing; but this new wine wouldn't make them violent or want to trash themselves or the town. Instead it would transform the way they lived their lives, causing them to engage more deeply with the world rather than escape it.

This Holy Spirit is a spirit that, once drunk, does not lead us to oblivion, but sets us free to greet the day with a full heart and a clear head.

22.5.2004

—

Saints and superheroes

These are confusing times. Islington Council is proposing that, when the St Mary Magdalene School in North London expands to become an academy, it should drop the word Saint from its name in case it causes offence to other religions. It's a curious request, particularly as the school has received £2 million in sponsorship from the Church of England, and as many of the Jewish and Muslim parents who have children at the school see nothing offensive in the school being named after a saint.

The council have suggested that the school be called the Islington Academy, or possibly the Magdalene Academy, which, they point out, retains the essentially Christian ethos of the school. Interestingly, there is no concern for the fact that the school will still be named after a demon-exorcized reformed prostitute, but that's a mere detail. Just as long as we get rid of the S word, all will be well.

If this idea catches on and the word saint is outlawed from all institutions in the land, there could be trouble. We'll have to rename all kinds of things: cities, hospitals, train stations, French football teams, anti-depressant herbs and fine clarets. We'll be drinking Emilion wine, catching trains from Pancras and taking summer holidays in Ives.

I wonder. Is the councillors' desire to drop the word really about tolerance for other religions, or is it another form of the secular coercion that forbids French muslim girls from wearing headscarves to school, or prevents children from saying prayers in assembly?

Names have associations, and there's no simpler way of removing those associations than changing the name. When Stalin renamed St Petersburg his action had more to with his loathing for things Christian than a belief that Leningrad was a catchier moniker.

The problem with the word saint is that it has lost something of its true meaning. These days a saint is either an archaic, aloof fanatic or an impossibly good person doing things people like you and me can never do. A saint is a member of an elite club that we are barred from entering, yet to be a saint is to be the very opposite of superior or elite. Nor is a saint someone who is impossibly good. A saint is really an ordinary person made exceptional by the transforming power of God.

Mary Magdalene is a potent reminder of this. Before her transformative encounter with Jesus, she was a desperate and despised woman, shunned by everyone. Even before Peter was a saint he was a lowly fisherman minding his own business. They were not looking to be saints. They weren't even looking to be changed.

Do we really want to live in a world without saints? The world needs saints. Not superheros. Just ordinary people who are open to the possibility that God can change them. Maybe retaining the word is a reminder of this potential. If the Mary Magdalene school in Islington keep the word saint in their title, it won't make the children better people, but it will be a reminder of the hope that the sacred brings; a hope that can change the most ordinary and least deserving person into someone who they still name schools after 2000 years later.

6.11.2004

—

How would Jesus vote?

In the run up to this US election a furious row has been underway as to which of the two parties' policies best reflect Christian values. There is even a website asking the question, who would Jesus vote for?

The Republicans – who see themselves as God's own party – seem in no doubt that their man would get the Lord's vote. They say you only have to look at Bush's stance on abortion, homosexuality and his personal commitment to Jesus to know this. Meanwhile, the Democrats – who have a quieter, but no less sincere core of believers – point to their own policies on poverty, the environment and peace as being more in keeping with the spirit of Christianity.

The message of Jesus has always been coerced by both right and left, from Baptists in Texas to the socialist priests in Peru. Yet in recent times, Christianity seems to have become so associated with American conservative politics that many neutral observers might be forgiven for thinking 'born again' meant Republican, and that 'biblical values' were a set of laws designed to give minorities a hard time.

Of course, if he were living now, Jesus wouldn't be allowed to vote because, as far as we know, he wasn't an American. Even if he were able to get a green card, switch nationality and get down to the polling station in Austin, can anyone say for sure which chad he would press?

Jesus was not right- or left-wing. His message was way more radical than any speech delivered by any politician in history. If his followers were expecting a political saviour they were to be disappointed. When Jesus stood up to deliver his own, low-cost campaign manifesto, instead of describing a great society in which all would be equal and happy, he gave them The Sermon on the Mount. This was no political utopia. When he talked about a shining city on a hill, it wasn't one built on corporate power, but one made up of people who were lost, sick and poor, but prepared to give themselves for his cause.

Some would have us believe that our future existence depends upon whether Kerry or Bush gets elected; but the fact is, this election will not transform the lives of ordinary Americans any more than it will change you and me. Politicians aren't in the business of transforming people – that is way beyond their remit; they can shape and frame policies that reform society, but they can't reform hearts and minds.

That was a mission Jesus took upon himself. For him the real power struggles didn't take place in the ballot box; they occurred in our inner being – for this is the place where we choose daily who will run our lives.

If we were able to ask Jesus how he'd vote in the US election, my guess is he'd turn the question round and ask us if we had voted for him yet? The great American folksinger Woodie Guthrie put it beautifully in a song that would later be set to music by Billy Bragg:

> "Let's have Christ for president, let's have him for our king,
> cast your vote for the carpenter you call the Nazarene,
> the only way we can ever beat the crooked politician men,
> is run the money changers out of the temple and put the
>   carpenter in."

15.11.2004

—

Agree to disagree

An old friend of mine rang me out the blue this week and, after about a minute, we landed on the subject of religion. My friend said to me: 'Rhid, why do you believe all that religious nonsense?' I was on a crowded tube but I couldn't stop myself. I began to subject my friend and my fellow commuters to a robust and increasingly irritable defence of my faith. The discussion got so involved that I over-shot my stop. Half an hour later, I arrived at my front door just as my friend was saying, 'We'll never ever agree on this subject. We'll just have to agree to disagree.'

I felt depressed that evening. I believed that what I said was right, but I hadn't said it in the right spirit. I had forgotten what mattered – I wanted to win the argument more than I wanted to relate to my friend. He had called me up to see how I was and I'd given him a sermon. We had quickly adopted our positions (in his corner, the view that there is no God, that life is random and that Jesus was just a man; and in my corner, the view that there is a God, that life has meaning and that Jesus is God).

We both landed telling blows, but the fight ended in a stalemate – pride bruised and no one taking the prize money. We may have agreed to disagree – but my real thought was that next time we talked on this subject I would knock his block off in the first round.

This has been a bumper week for religious arguments: members of Christian Voice damning the cast of Gerry Springer; newspaper columnists damning the religious right for not wanting homosexuals in the priesthood; and it's all characterized by the same polarization of view and inability to hear what the other person actually believes. These are fast becoming subjects upon which we can no longer agree to disagree. When that happens the conversation comes to an end; we divide into the right and the wrong. With ourselves, of course, always in the right.

Agreeing to disagree is a vital law for life, it's the only way we can live with differing views. It does not mean we give assent to things we believe to be wrong, but if, in the midst of arguing our case, we put people down, hate or pronounce judgement on others, then we've blown it.

Jesus won this argument for good when at the public stoning of a sinner he put his finger in the sand, drew a line and invited those who considered themselves perfect enough to step over it. No one moved because no one had the credentials. Not only was he showing that we are to love rather than judge, he demonstrated that we cannot love adequately unless we are prepared to lose the right to be right.

Paul develops this in Philippians: 'Be like minded, having the same love… do nothing out of vain conceit, but in humility consider others better than yourselves. Your attitude should be the same as Jesus who being in the very nature god, did not consider equality with God something to be grasped… but made himself nothing.'

The next time my friend rings I need to remember this. I need to forget about winning the argument and being right. Maybe I just need to say nothing in order to connect with the person at the other end of the line.

26.2.2005

—

Hoodies

A few years ago there was a commercial for a newspaper in which a man with a shaved head is seen charging up a street looking like he's about to do some serious damage; the action cuts to a terrified woman clutching her handbag and it seems certain that the skinhead is going to rob her; until we see the action from a different angle and notice that a pile of bricks is about to tumble onto the street and the man is actually going to save the woman from injury.

The ad brilliantly illustrates the dangers of judging by appearances, and in the light of the recent reaction to our 'yob culture', it would be good if they could re-run it, substituting the clothes of the skinhead for the uniform of today's supposed most likely offender – the hooded sweatshirt and baseball cap. It might help us think again about judging groups of people based on what they wear.

Ever since Adam and Eve pulled on breeches there's been a connection between wrong-doing and covering up. Hoods keep your ears warm, but they can also protect your identity if you want to engage in criminal activity. How else do you think Robin Hood – the original hoody (or hoodlum) – got away with it? As my hoody-wearing son would tell you, good guys and bad guys wear hoods. For every Sith Lord about to destroy the universe there's an Obi-Wan Kenobi battling to save it.

The most evil regimes in history have worn the smartest uniforms. Indeed, you could make a strong case for the most criminal group of people in this country being suit wearers: isn't it people in suits who are largely responsible for robbing pension schemes, selling arms to countries that can't afford them and starting wars?

Scripture has some helpful advice on clothing (don't worry about what you wear; and don't judge people by what they wear); but it's what's going on beneath the dark hoods, the fine robes or the Armani suits that really counts. Clothes are a poor gauge of someone's character or intentions. God notices behaviour before he notices clothes; inner adornment before outer.

The intimidating behaviour of kids in shopping centres is not to be defended; but instead of threatening to exchange their hoods for orange penal suits, maybe we should be asking why they behave in the way they do. Is all the anger, boredom and frustration that roams the nation remedied by a change of clothes?

In some ways, I suspect that these kids are not so different to us. They're probably even asking the same questions: How can I enjoy myself? What's it all for? What is real? The people abusing shoppers are not so different to the shoppers who harm themselves buying things they don't need and can't afford. Perhaps, they're just medicating the emptiness in different ways.

Dissatisfaction with life and a lack of purpose is a spiritual issue before it is an economic or social one. If we really are spiritual beings, wired for relationship, for fulfilment, for meaning, then we are only going to be moved and changed by spiritual answers; answers that education, culture and politics are limited at providing. If meaning and reality is found in God, then everything else is killing time.

When the prophet Isaiah wrote that 'Before God our righteous actions are but rags', he was saying that no matter what we do or wear, in a fundamental way, we are all dressed the same. We are all in need of new clothing and only God can clothe us as we should be clothed.

17.5.2005

—

It was 20 years ago today (For Live 8)

Good morning, good morning, good morning,
London Calling, to the far away town...
It was twenty years ago today,
And we've still got something to say
Not talking about London, Paris, New York, Munich.
Talking about my generation
There's a feeling I get when I look to the West. And it makes me wonder.
Where is my beautiful car? Where is my beautiful house.
I want it now; I want it all. I want money.
Get back. I'm all right Jack; keep your hands off my stack.
Money, it's a crime. Share it fairly but don't take a slice of my pie.
I read the news today, oh boy,
Mother, Mother, there's too many of you crying,
Brother, Brother, Brother there's far too many of you dying.
Help I need somebody
I'm just a poor boy nobody loves me...
Them belly full but them hungry.
You never give me your money, you only give me your funny paper...
Help me get my feet back on the ground – won't you please, please
    help me

Don't leave me here all alone. Helpless. Helpless. Helpless
Don't walk on by
Ticking away the moments that make up a dull day,
Fritter and waste the hours in an off hand way.
'Cos maybe, you're going to be the one that saves me.
There are still many rivers to cross and I still can't find my way over
Sometimes you can't make it on your own.
Don't give up, 'cos you have friends...
Imagine
Life is bigger; it's bigger than you
Consider this, the hint of the century
The world is full of refuges, a lot like you and a lot like me.
War is not the answer. You don't have to escalate. Only love can conquer hate.
It's easy if you try.
Come on everybody. Mr President. Come on. Come on. Let's go.
Jesus loves you more than you will know.
But it's a hard road to follow and rough tough way to go.
What you going to do about it, what you going to do?
Nothing to do, it's up to you
You can't always get what you want,
But if you try sometimes, you get what you need.
Get up, stand up, stand up for your rights.
With or without you
Give a little bit. Give a little bit of my life for you.
While you see your chance, take it.
Are you such a dreamer, to put the world to rights?
Dry your eyes mate. We can be heroes just for one day.
Today is gonna' to be the day that they're gonna' throw it back to you.
By now you should have found out you realise what you gotta' do.
Time to make the change, come on you rock and rollers.
Look at the stars see how they shine for you
With the boys from the Mersey and the Thames and the Tyne...

All the people, so many people, and they all go hand in hand, hand
    in hand
Nothing to say but what a day
It's going to be a glorious day.
A beautiful day
I can feel it coming in the air tonight, O Lord...
Won't you help to sing these songs of freedom
Redemption songs
Right here right now
You know we've got to find a way
To bring some loving here today.
And in the end, the love you take is equal to the love you make.

2.7.2005

—

Cricket, lovely cricket

Good morning, or as the doyen of cricket commentary, Ritchie
Benaud, will be saying in two and half hours: 'Morning everyone.'

Yes, the fifth test between England and Australia starts today. The
final match of a series that many are saying has been the greatest ever;
a clash so intense and exciting that it has threatened the number one
status of our national religion, football. The sponsors of the series are
even inviting us to sing Jerusalem for the boys as they step onto the
hallowed turf.

Cricket has many of the right ingredients for a religion. It has men
wearing hats, arcane rules and bizarre names, which only a select
few are able to understand. It has someone called a twelfth man, a
council that decides doctrine, and a shrine at a place called Lords.
It even has its own sacred text: Wisden. Unofficially described as
'The Bible of Cricket,' it weighs as much as a Bible and contains just

as many unpronounceable names. Can it be mere coincidence that the great plinth at Stonehenge is exactly 22 yards away from the dolmen whose shape is reminiscent of a set of stumps and bails?

Like religion, cricket can also be hard to appreciate, tedious and require only our nominal attention. It was Lord Mancroft who wrote that it was a game the English, not being spiritual people, had invented to give themselves some concept of eternity. It certainly seems like an eternity since we last won the Ashes.

Indeed, not so long ago it looked as if cricket – like the official state religion – was dying in the mother country and thriving in the nations that had been proselytized. I once stood on a beach in Antigua listening to a local wearing a T-shirt that said 'cricket lovely cricket' – describing Viv Richards as 'a god in his own right.' This week the orthodox Australian Prime Minister appeared on television considering the effect that defeat would have on the nation's spirits; in India, which has the highest number of devotees, the game has the ability to postpone weddings, close parliament early and unify Sikhs, Hindus and Muslims – some believe that standing in the field all day has had some influence on the practise of meditation.

Things are different now. We're in the middle of a revival, an outpouring of fervour that's not been seen since, well, since The Great Revival. We've seen whole villages transformed overnight, men give up their usual ways and even some women converted. We have witnessed discipline and commitment. Applauded grace under pressure. Raised our voices in passionate unison – things we might have once expected from our religious practices. Perhaps this revival shows there's a hunger there – an appetite that will always find ways to be fed.

And if England lose this match? We can always blame the weather… and we all know who's responsible for that.

8.9.2005

A glass of water

This Thought comes to you from rural Kenya where we have been living for the last month.

Although we are a well-travelled family, we have rarely been to places where people live on the dollar a day that a third of the world's population try to survive on. If we ever witnessed this poverty it was fleeting and at best made an edgy 'authentic' snap for our photo album. We didn't dare to experience what it was like to live alongside serious deprivation. That was something for anthropologists and priests. We were busy pursuing culture and recreation. For isn't this how we learn about the world?

Living in a community, with a high prevalence of HIV/Aids, a water shortage, no electricity, unreliable food and exceptionally bad roads, has seriously challenged our understanding about the world. We can't help feeling that if we'd done this earlier we might have learned things that years of pursuing culture and pleasure have failed to teach us.

Not that when you come to Africa you expect to be taught something. If anything, you think, because you've read the economic arguments and know the history, and come from a part of the world which has surely worked out how life works, that you have something to teach it.

Then you get to this massive, red-earthed continent and, away from the tourist bubble, you realize that your horizons have been utterly limited until now, and that these people you characterized as poor and sick and somehow lacking in the basics are, despite all they face, talented, funny and generous; that they live with exceptional hope and resilience, and in communities so inter-dependent that is makes our individualistic, self-sufficient lives seem deleterious. For a while, your whole system for measuring 'wealth' gets turned upside down.

Then you wake up the next day and circumstances douse your naïve enthusiasm: across the road a 35-year-old man dies of AIDS, leaving five more orphans for the community to feed; then you learn that the community has inadequate water for crops because there's been a two-year drought; then a tearful father asks you for funds to send a daughter to secondary school; and there is a scandal about the government spending millions on fleets of flashy four wheel drives, a government that is already spending more on repaying debt than it does on education – and you want to push your head into the red dust and scream.

The next day the sun comes up, and you see the people walking to market to sell mangoes and goats in exchange for exercise books and tools; and in church people pledge sacks of beans for the orphans; and the widows group are using the money from their maize to buy another cow; and maybe the government are going to bore for water after all, and there's sense that, with a little support and some investment that this could all work…

You sit down exhausted from the rollercoaster of an African day, when your 70-year-old neighbour comes to check that you are okay (as if you are the one who is deprived) and you offer her a glass of water and she pauses before drinking and you wonder if you've broken some social protocol; then you see that she is actually thanking God for the glass of the water and for the gift of life, and you realize that all your wealth, travel, education and privilege has never really taught you the true worth of a glass of water or been able to demonstrate how precious life is as simply and powerfully as this.

2.2.2006

—

Slum God

Yesterday, we went to one of the biggest slums in the world, the Kibera, here in Nairobi. My guidebook says the population of Nairobi is two million. This is odd, because the estimated population of the slum is three million. In fact, the guide doesn't mention the Kibera at all.

It simply says: 'Nairobi has scenes of shocking poverty, so if you are worried stay in one of the affluent suburbs rather than the downtown dives.' It effortlessly ignores the Kibera, and by extension the existence of three million people, before directing people to the country's wildlife. Which is a pity because a short visit to the Kibera will show you as much life – wild and tame – as any safari.

Anyway, the Kibera does exist and so do its people. Just follow the signs from the city centre and you'll come to a copper-coloured, shanty city filling a 5km gulley. Of the city's population, 60 per cent live on five per cent of the land. We'd actually seen this place in the film *The Constant Gardner*, but even a gritty, authentic movie can't quite capture the sensory assault. The definition of a slum as 'an overcrowded area of a city in which the housing is in very bad condition' doesn't quite cut it.

Entering Kibera – like the slums of Mumbai last month – I had a series of reactions, from the indignant, 'How on earth can people live like this?' to the amazed. 'Look how alive this place is.' For a moment you almost feel envy at the anarchic connectedness of the community and the fact that the people look happier than back in the capital's smart coffee bars.

Then you walk deeper into the community, over mountains of ordure, and you realize that behind the smiles there is a daily battle going on that NGOs providing toilets can't alleviate and the indignation returns. Surely a society that has the wit and the will to put a cup of latte on a table, but one mile from here, can find a way to clear the garbage that kills people every day; or surely a country like India, that makes claims for superpower status, could actually use its garbage to fuel its economy instead of going nuclear? Where is the connection between the deals done by statesmen and this struggle for daily living? When are we going to measure the greatness of nations by the way they treat their poorest instead of by the kilowatts of power they generate?

A slum says many things. The danger for us is that if we don't like what we hear we disconnect: we make sure the presidential plane avoids the slum side of the city, we fail to mention them in our books; we do our bit, then walk away. I confess that after a few hours of walking through the Kibera, with the rain beginning to fall, I wanted to get away. I was worried about the dirt on my daughter's feet and the drunk man hassling my son for money.

Amazingly there are people in the world who subvert this disconnection. We were being shown around by just such a group from the Salvation Army – people who believe that one of the best way to help people is to be with them. The world's slums are lit up with people like this, people who believe that the way to bring change to a community is to be present whatever the conditions. Then maybe it is easier to do this when you believe in a God who chose to be born in a pig's sty and die on a hill of decaying garbage in order to remain connected.

8.3.2006

—

Only God can forgive this

Today marks the twelfth Anniversary of the genocide in Rwanda. When I arrived in Rwanda with my family last month we were full of nerves. Stepping on to land where 800,000 people were killed in 100 days makes you wary.

Yet first you discover a land so beautiful that you wonder if this really is the place where one of the world's worst atrocities happened, and other issues seem far more pressing, namely the grinding poverty. The World Bank estimates that 21 per cent of the world's population live on less than a dollar a day; for Rwanda their latest government statistics make it 69 per cent!

Then you meet the people and you get a sense of terrible things done not so long ago. The old – of whom there are noticeably few –

greet us with warmth, amazed that we are here; while the younger generations seem far more reticent.

Tentatively, you start to ask questions, but the teacher at the school doesn't want to talk about it; neither does the captain in the Salvation Army we are with. Only after a week do we learn that her father was killed after refusing to leave his village.

On the third day we met a Spanish priest who had been here for 40 years. His eyes soon fill with tears as he tells us that he reluctantly left during the genocide. When he returned, half his congregation were dead. I asked him what a man who follows Jesus preaches in such a situation. 'First he must talk of justice,' he says, 'reconciliation is too hard without this.' Yet it's only forgiveness that enables people to move forward, and in an extreme situation like this, forgiveness is not an act of the intellect, or even of the heart; it is an act of will. You have to choose it if you want to move on. In scripture, it says God not only forgives our transgressions, He forgets them. However, this is hard for man to do. The next day we visit a prison full of genocide suspects; a place where the complicated process of man's justice slowly works itself out. Again we arrive with trepidation. Yet our anxiety is mocked by the site of inmates dressed in pink uniforms. As my son says, it's a colour that helps you see them as people rather than murderers. Within minutes we are smiling and waving and talking with men who had more than likely murdered others; men who would have been boys at the time of the genocide; boys not much older than my son.

Then we arrive at the Genocide Museum in Kigali and you are shown that genocide is nothing new, rare or random. That it is usually planned. All you need is an oppressed people, manipulative leaders and an enemy. As you leave the museum you read the well-intentioned words 'never again' and agree, still conscious that genocide is happening again, right now and in a country not that far away.

On the last day of our stay, we meet a woman who seemed to embody this need to remember and forgive, to lament and to hope; a woman who lost a husband and her children, but who is now leading a group of widows, some of them supposed former enemies. How does she manage to do this? I ask her and she looks at me for the first time. 'I can only do this with God', she says, 'because only God has forgiven us without conditions'.

6.4.2006

—

Forbidden faith

At the entrance to the Forbidden City the image of Mao Zedong stares out towards Tiananmen Square, over the crowds who have come to see one of China's prized treasures. My son wanted to know why there was still a picture of this man hanging in such pride of place. I said maybe the people still revere him. Or perhaps they don't know what he did and are not ready to face up to it. China is moving so fast towards its new future there seems to be no time for assessing the past; which is interesting as the former Chairman himself said, 'I don't know about the past; I don't know about the future. They have nothing to do with the reality of my own self.'

My son's observation made me think: who or what creed is this great nation looking to for inspiration now that the old beliefs have been tried? What a man – or a nation – believes determines the fruit they bear. Mao offers absolute proof of this; he once wrote, 'the country must first of all be destroyed and then reformed' – a belief that led to a peacetime death toll of 70 million and a nation once famed for its intellectual creativity being coerced into a period of collective brain death.

There are startling signs that this creativity is being reborn. Only this time the spark isn't Marx or Lenin. If anything, the new creed is one most of us seem to worship – The Market. Right now, China is a country moving so fast it takes your breath away – literally in the case of Beijing, a city building at breakneck speed, with traffic so thick it made me nostalgic for the M25. This souped-up development isn't unique to the capital; it's happening in every city from Ghuanzou to Shanghai.

Out in the country, we came across a different kind of power at work. In the ancient, central province of Henan, we visited an area that had been devastated by the HIV/AIDS pandemic that broke out 15 years ago when impoverished farmers sold blood for money; blood that was never properly screened and led to an estimated 200,000 infections.

Because of the political sensitivities, it was a rare privilege to even be allowed to meet these people. The villages we saw were poor, as poor as anything we have seen on this journey, but the people we met were generous and open, inviting us into their homes and showing us how they had found a will to live. After a few of these visits I began to notice a pattern: instead of being decorated with pictures of Mao, nearly every house we visited had a cross or a picture of Jesus hanging in pride of place.

Mao's wife, Jiang Qing, once pronounced that Christianity in China had been consigned to the museum. She obviously hadn't counted on the underground church. Henan is the epicentre of China's house church movement and conservative estimates put the number of Christians in China at 90 million. I can't verify this number – official statistics for anything are hard to come by here, especially awkward ones – yet in these villages we met people whose lives had clearly been transformed; not by government slogans, or by political maxims, nor even the burgeoning market; they had been given new hope because of faith.

Mao had once written, 'People like me only have a duty to ourselves; we have no duty to other people.' These Christians in China seem to have other ideas.

12.7.2006

Home

I have just returned with my family from an eight-month journey that took us into the heartlands of the HIV/AIDS epidemic. It's good to be home. Although it is a bit weird. Part of the strangeness is to do with feeling a tension between appreciating the familiarity and comfort of home while sensing that these things are not as essential to our happiness and security as we thought they were.

For the last eight months we have lived in other people's homes: some big houses, some cramped apartments, hostels, hotels, a tent; places without power, hot water and even toilets; often we slept in one room together. The only consistent aspect of family life was that all four of us were together, every day. The accommodation kept changing, but it was us, with our three bags, trumpet and lap top who provided the stability. Wherever we laid our luggage, that was our home.

Towards the end of the journey, someone asked me if we were looking forward to getting home and I surprised myself when I answered that I felt I already was home, because we were it. The thing made of bricks back in London – albeit a thing I am grateful for – was really just a house.

So it proved when we stepped across the threshold of the place we call home. It actually felt as if we were bringing home back to the house rather than the other way round. The confirmation that our settlement was not our ultimate security was oddly liberating.

It was also salutary, coming back to a culture that stakes so much of its time, money and thought-life on property. As we set out on a massive campaign of DIY, I kept telling myself: taking care of your house is the responsible thing to do, but don't construct your happiness around this. By the second week, panelling my house was making me restless.

Maybe this restlessness is a good thing. There is something in us that senses – even longs for – a home we haven't quite found yet. The Apostle Paul put it this way: 'Now we know that if the earthly tent we live in is destroyed, we have a building from God, an eternal house not built by human hands. We groan, longing to be clothed with our heavenly dwelling.'

Being away helped us appreciate that home is an elusive, invisible thing; yet something more permanent than the brick walls we live behind. The experience of impermanence took us closer to a possible truth that our real security comes from knowing that we all have a home that is eternal.

Two of the most secure people I met on the journey were a couple in India who lived in a home the same size as my bathroom. It was beautiful in its own way and they were proud of it, but the secret of their contentment clearly wasn't connected to their square meterage. They lived in this tiny space, but their life was somewhere else. Their hopes fixed on another kind of dwelling.

8.9.2006

—

A state of corruption

When you walk past a man in the street who begs you for money it's easy not to give it to him. You've already calculated that he will spend it on drink, or worse. His state of corruption is too entrenched. You figure that giving him the money won't change anything; that there are better ways of spending it. Anyway, he got himself into that state. It's not your problem.

This is a microcosm of the situation faced by governments of rich countries trying to decide whether to give money to poor ones. We make the same judgements. We say: 'Maybe if that country cleans up its act, we will give money, but until that happens it's staying in our pockets.'

This question of conditionality and giving is one that Hilary Benn, the international development secretary, has raised this week. Benn believes that the World Bank have made it almost impossible for governments of poor nations to meet the conditions asked of them. In protest at the onerous requirements, Britain is withholding £50 million of its funding.

Benn's argument is a simple one: we should not walk away from our responsibilities to the poor, whatever the behaviour of their politicians. Yes, let's encourage good governance and let's not give money to countries who spend the money on weapons or corporate favours (good job we're not a poor country); but let's not penalize the people who need the money most, simply because we assume they are part of the corruption.

A friend of mine who worked for an NGO in Mali said he spent months trying to convince donors to drop the conditions they had in place and to trust the people who needed the money to spend it well. Because they didn't, the money sat in an account doing nothing. Eventually he managed to get some funds to a small group of women in a remote community who had so far failed to meet the stringent criteria imposed. In one month they utterly transformed the life of the village; all because someone ignored the prejudice and took a chance on them.

Every day they read about government scandal, powerless to do anything about it despite having voted them in. Should they be penalized for their leaders' failures? Particularly when we have left such a poor legacy of governance ourselves. Travelling through Africa this year it was hard not to believe that the corruption of public life has some roots in what we and other colonialist powers did. It's a failure of understanding to say 'it's their problem.'

In Kenya I met a group of 80-years-olds who had worked most of their lives for an English tobacco farmer. It was a rare opportunity to ask people what life was like before they were colonized. One of them spoke. Without rancour he said: 'You brought poverty, you took our land, took away our freedom of expression, you destroyed our family life and stole our time.' It was a painful speech to hear, but he wasn't done. He added, 'But someone brought the gospel and because of that we can forgive you.'

If they can forgive us for our corruption, can't we at least return the grace?

15.9.2006

—

Sex worker

A few months ago I went to a brothel in Mumbai. I was with Nishikant Ranaware who worked with the Salvation Army looking after the children of sex workers. I wasn't really prepared for what we stepped into. Art and literature had glamorized my ideas of what a brothel might look like; an amalgam of Mata Hari, Toulouse Lautrec and Dodge City saloons had me thinking of lace and perfume. Yet this was no palace of delights. It was a house where the pathetic endgames of desire and abuse play themselves out. At one end of the corridor a boy – the same age as my son – sat staring at nothing while in the room behind him a man went with his mother for the price of a loaf of bread. At the far end of the house, a madam sat watching over a two-week old baby who lay in a little patch of light coming through a hole in the wall. A baby born in a brothel and, being a girl, destined to remain in one.

There is absolutely nothing glamorous about sex work. Calling it the oldest profession in the world is a kind of obfuscation that keeps us from facing up to what's really behind it. Prostitution is usually a state where addiction, abuse and relational dysfunction all meet and make a transaction. Many of the life stories of the women who have been murdered in Ipswich attest to this, and their deaths are a vicious reminder of the truth that it is women who take the greatest risks and bear the burden of a 'vice' for which men create a demand.

Standing in that Mumbai brothel, with a just-born baby girl, I asked myself the question: where is the hope for this baby, and for these women? Nishikant was not overwhelmed. He invited the other women to join us in the tiny room and he said a prayer. The infant was still asleep. It was an unlikely setting for a blessing, but then we were offering a prayer to a God who was born in a place not much more salubrious than this; to a teenage girl who had conceived out of wedlock; a baby whose genealogy included several abused women, among them Rahab and Tamar who both sold themselves for sex.

Christmas is an oppressively sentimental time of year, but it shouldn't be. Sentiment is a kind of prostitution: a selling short of the truth for a quick, good feeling. If we look at the nativity and see only tinsel and presents and not the helpless, naked baby or the pig manure, then we've missed it. Do we really believe that a scrap of humanity, born in a manger, can be the hope for the world? When I think of people like Nishikant expressing that in-carnational love in the darkest of places, it makes this mystery a little easier to believe.

15.12.2006

—

Education of the soul

I was once at a party where a man came up to me and said: 'I'll talk about anything, but if you mention schools, I'll have to kill you.' He was at the end of his tether talking to neurotic parents about where their child was going to be educated. I said I hoped I wouldn't become one of those people.

Now I am becoming one of those people and I'm particularly annoyed with myself. I thought travel had inoculated me against that particular disease. After discovering that secondary education is a luxury most of the world can't afford, I made a vow: I will not worry if my son doesn't get to the school we want. At least he has a school to go to.

On the day we are due to find out which school my son is going to, I'm a bag of nerves. 'Please God,' I pray, 'let him get the school he wants,' i.e. not the one next to his primary school, that would be perfect if it were any good; but the one a bus-ride away, that used to be bad but is, according to league-tables, getting better.

Buried in my prayer I could hear the undoing of all the lessons I thought I'd learned; all the ideals I'd formed – about education being about experience, community, friendship – disappearing in the urge to protect my own.

When we took our children out of school to travel through countries affected by AIDS, people said: 'What a wonderful education that'll be for them.' Thus it proved: in the morning they'd be home-schooled; in the afternoon, they'd go to the funeral of a man who'd died of a disease he'd got from sleeping around. It wasn't stuff you'd find on the curriculum, but it felt like preparation for something.

In all the deranged scramble over school admissions, it's helpful just to stop and ask a naïve question: what is a good education?

Richard Ruhr, a Franciscan priest, who did a comparative study of initiation rites, discovered a remarkable similarity in the 'lessons of life' that such rites attempt to teach the young. He summarized them as follows: 'Life is hard. You're going to die. You're not that important. You're not in control. Life is not just about you.' They sound harsh and yet each one contains a spiritual truth, and a truth best grasped early. Yet it seems that in our culture we want to hide these truths, especially from our children. So we feed them: 'Life can be easy. You can stay young forever. You are what's most important. You must stay in control. Life is mostly about you and your fulfilment.'

Schools could be a part of a counter-culture: places founded not on the belief that life is a lottery or a good education is just for a privileged enclave, but on the principle that every child should have the opportunity to develop their whole moral and intellectual potential. As a teacher at Ampleforth School, Dom Anthony Sutch said that he was really *preparing his pupils for death*.

Education isn't just an intellectual and moral training, it's about engaging with the great realities: Love, Death and God; it's an education of the soul. That's something that no league table or admissions board could ever measure.

2.3.2007

—

The comedian versus the scientist

A spat has emerged this week between two unlikely opponents: in the deep-blue, serious corner the heavyweight evolutionary biologist Richard Dawkins; and in the red-nosed, slightly less serious corner the heavyweight comedian Peter Kay.

The comedian and the scientist are rivals for a book award in which Dawkins's *The God Delusion* and Kay's *The Sound of Laughter* are both entries. In his memoir Kay writes: 'I believe in a God of some kind, in some sort of higher being. Personally, I find it comforting.' After reading this, Dawkins asked: 'How can you take seriously someone who likes to believe something because he finds it comforting?'

Now I'm not sure Kay is aiming to be taken seriously. This is the man who delivered the nation's favourite one-liner: 'Garlic bread – it's the future, I've tasted it.' However, Richard Dawkins has a good point. Belief in such an important possibility should be founded on more than a feeling. He's not just questioning the existence of God, but more the nature of the comfort that people get from having such a vague belief. Dawkins himself is reported as saying that 'If there was evidence for a supreme being he would change his mind – with pride and great surprise – but he doubts whether the revelation would be comforting.'

Scripture itself has some uncomforting things to say about comfort and some uncomfortable things to say about God. It has Job dismissing 'the miserable comforters,' with their whistling in the dark platitudes of 'oh don't worry, it'll all work out.' David, who when in distress said, 'I remembered you God and I groaned.' In the end the only comfort that sufficed for Job was his conviction that God was real.

Peter Kay has a point, too. There is, it seems, some undeniable connection between belief in this God and the comfort that it brings. If scripture is the fossil record of a people's interaction with this God, there is a seam of comfort running all the way through the story. People even call him 'the God of all comfort.'

The idea that faith is just a seeking after comfort is a variation on the idea that faith is a crutch. C. S. Lewis' one liner reply to this was: 'I don't need a crutch I need an ambulance.' He was making a serious point: admission of our need and brokenness is the starting point of faith in a God who has already entered into this suffering.

Peter Kay – who was educated at a Catholic school – doesn't expand on the nature of the supreme being in his book, but he does express doubt about the divinity of Jesus, seeing him as 'just an ordinary man, like you and me.' It's interesting that he finds a belief in a supreme being comforting and yet for him there's no connection between Jesus and that supreme being. After all, when Jesus told the disciples he was going to die a painful death, he said he would ask the Father to send them another comforter – 'the spirit of truth.' It was as if, for him, comfort and truth were the same things.

9.3.2007

—

100 years of attitude

On the day that people were rushing to purchase the latest and supposedly greatest anti-wrinkle cream from Boots the chemist, I went to the funeral of my step-grandmother, Wyn, who had died a few days shy of her 101st birthday.

Those of us looking for tips on longevity and creaseless aging weren't going to get much conventional wisdom from Grany Wyn: she had taken up smoking when she was 60. If she had used anti-wrinkle cream it was too late to get her money back.

The order of service card had two photographs: one depicting her in her prime, clear skinned and conventionally beautiful; the other showing her at 100, smoking a cigarette, the wrinkles on her hands and face like maps of the century she'd lived through.

A quote she loved written next to the photograph said: 'Life should not be a journey to the grave with the intention of arriving safely in an attractive and well-preserved body.' As it was, Wyn was blessed with a strong enough body to live through an entire century – including two world wars.

Here's the paradox: her amazingly long life made the celebration easier, but it couldn't anaesthetize death's sting. As my brother said, her being 100 makes the hole bigger. The ultimate question was still hanging over the coffin in the crematorium chapel, and it took one of her great-grandchildren to ask it: Where has Gran gone?

My unconventional Gran was perhaps more typical than she realized on the religious question. As the vicar who took the service was gracious enough to remind us: Win believed in God but she disliked 'church and all that claptrap.' Yet even my iconoclastic, vicar-dodging grandmother could not (maybe did not want to) throw out the Baby Jesus with the bathwater.

The service aimed for somewhere between a rejection of ritual and the need to express a hope in a life to come. Taking in both the Gentle Jesus prayer and the poem about death being like going to the next room. Was this sentimental hedging; or was it Gran's statement of faith?

I have yet to attend a funeral where someone says of death: 'That's it. No more meeting again. That's the end.' Is this because the thought of total annihilation and separation from those we love is too painful; or is it because a hope in something beyond this life is embedded deep in all of us?

The 'vicar who shouldn't have been there' was doing a good job of holding these things in tension (I was beginning to think Gran would have liked him) when he offered the kernel of an answer from Ecclesiastes, which says: 'God plants eternity in the hearts of men.' As if to say the expectation of a life beyond this life is already hot-wired into our DNA.

Perhaps a clue to what happens in the next life can be found in the love we feel for those who have left us. It's not religion that enables us to leap across death's divide, but love – for as it says in Romans, 'Nothing – not death, not life, will be able to separate us from the love of God.' Not even a dislike of vicars, ritual and 'all that claptrap.'

8.5.2007

—

'Why do the wicked live on?'

A year ago I was standing in the Harare Cricket Ground bar watching the FA Cup Final on TV and for a few hours, the narcotic effect of beer and sport made it possible to forget where you were. The only clue that this was a country in deep trouble was the price of the beer which, at $600,000 Zim a pint, cost as much as a three-bedroomed house had done when Robert Mugabe came to power. At half time a man next to me said, you know what is wrong with Zimbabwe? It's the IMF.'

'The IMF? Why?' I asked.

He looked around, just in case anyone was listening: 'IMF: It's Mugabe's Fault.'

Being just half a mile from the presidential palace, this was a more daring joke than it sounded.

Meanwhile, a year on, safe in that guarded palace, the President lives on. Whatever Mugabe's achievements in earlier years, I can't help but be reminded of Job's question: 'Why do the wicked live on, growing old and increasing in power?' It's a horribly pertinent in a country where the average life expectancy has plummeted to 39 under the abuses of a leader who, at 82, is still fit and well and intending to hold on until at least 2010. He's partly done it by making his people compliant. Orwell wrote that people living under a dictatorship train themselves to stop noticing; by depriving his people of food and freedom and keeping them afraid, Mugabe has got them policing themselves. When I asked my taxi driver why they put up with it he said the people were too tired and afraid to do anything and that Zimbabweans were a peaceful people: 'Getting rid of Mugabe would mean bloodshed and we don't have the stomach for blood.'

Perhaps the lack of obvious, visceral conflict in Zimbabwe explains Mugabe's staying power. The violence is not as brutal as it is in Darfur; the streets are not running with the blood of Baghdad. It's easier for us to rage and talk of intervention when we are presented with the beaten and defiant face of a Morgan Tsvangirai, but harder to react when all we hear is the stifled silence of a people too worn down to help themselves. In a world that bombards us with anguished cries, the despairing moans of the Zimbabwean people have not been noisy enough.

'Those who have ears hear let them hear,' said Jesus. It's almost as if to hear the pain we need to attune ourselves, filter the noise and not be lulled into thinking things are not so bad because there's a lack of drama. The news that John Howard, the Australian Prime Minister, is stopping his country's cricket team from touring Zimbabwe in September is timely. Howard doesn't want to give Mugabe – whom he describes as 'a grubby dictator' – any reason to relax. He isn't going to add to the illusion that all is well in Zimbabwe by letting his compatriots play cricket there while its people suffer. This protest may seem like small beer, but it is still an answer to God's question 'who is hearing the cries of my people?' I believe we who are free to see and hear, need to amplify the voices of people whose cries can barely be heard.

15.5.2007

—

Caught on camera

In 1984, in the days before Orwellian CCTV cameras and smoking bans in pubs, I took a packet of 20 Silk Cut from the bar where I was working, telling myself I was merely borrowing the cigarettes against my wages and would pay for them that Friday. Friday came and when I arrived to do my evening shift, the landlord said he'd seen me steal the fags and was firing me. When I pleaded that I always intended to pay for them he said he didn't believe me. He had seen me popping a packet in my top pocket and looking over my shoulder to see if anyone was watching. Any inner deal I'd done with myself was my business. From his point of view, I was a thief.

Nowadays, I'd probably have been spotted and condemned by a CCTV camera – or perhaps verbally admonished by one. Big Brother it seems is not only watching you – he's telling you how to behave. Britain's first 'talking' CCTV cameras have just been trialed in Middlesborough. The system allows operators who spot anti-social acts to send out a verbal warning to people about to commit a wrong-doing. Apparently, people are so ashamed and embarrassed at being publicly berated that they slink off without causing further trouble. It makes people think twice.

How I wish I'd had a talking camera to stop me taking those cigarettes back in that fateful year. To have had someone shout 'Stop. Smoking cigarettes is bad for you and stealing them is worse!' But I'm not sure it would have got to the heart of the issue. Even now, after re-examining the footage of my own memory, I can't recall exactly what my real intentions were. I like to think I would have paid for those cigarettes if the landlord hadn't spotted me; but I can't be certain. Have I been trying to justify myself all these years? It's as if the CCTV cameras trained on my heart – or conscience, or wherever it is the soul resides – fail to penetrate deep enough. If we can't fully fathom our hearts, then who can?

It was Jeremiah who gives us God's question: 'Can anyone hide in secret places, so that I can not see him?' Back in 1984 I didn't really believe in an omniscient God. I had a vague sense of being watched, but the being I imagined watching me was more akin to a controller in a CCTV station trying to catch me out, rather than the God whom I have later learned knows me better than myself.

If our idea of God is limited to that of a penalizing controller, watching and waiting to condemn our every move, then we'll live fearful lives. We'll duck and dive from view and constantly look to how things appear outwardly. Yet if we believe in a God who is searching for truth in the inward parts and who allows us the freedom to make mistakes – even those we committed years ago – then we'll be able to walk with our heads up, unafraid of whoever else is watching us.

21.5.2007

—

Sub-prime people

While re-mortgaging last month I discovered that I fall into a newly defined category of human being. Formerly my mortgage, designed for people who are self-employed, was called a self-certification mortgage; now – thanks to a financial crisis – it's sub-prime.

We may not be able to predict the outcome of the current crises, but it's certainly adding to our vocabulary– words that were known only to financial institutions in Milwaukee now slip effortlessly into our conversation. None more so than the slightly sinister adjective, 'sub-prime.'

According to the US Department of Treasury, sub-prime borrowers 'typically display reduced payment capacity.' Or, to put it another way, they don't have much money. It's hard not to hear in this definition echoes of other demeaning stereotypes – America's poor white trash, or our own council house and violent chavs. It's perhaps why certain financial practices and product names hide behind euphemism: in warfare we have 'collateral damage' to describe innocent people killed in a military operation; in the financial world banks sell loans to people who can't afford them; then package the debt and define it as an asset. It's a fudging that allows us to avoid saying what a thing really is. As the economist Galbraith put it: 'The study of money is one in which complexity is used to disguise truth.'

The trouble is, our whole system seems to operate on debt. So much so that it's seen as naïve or unfashionable to question it. Being in the red is the new black. Even though many of us with a mortgage (a term that originally meant death pledge) know full well that when we fill out a form asking us if we are a home owner, we are so merely for the purposes of filling out the form. Home borrower doesn't sound quite – well – 'prime' enough.

Could it be that the creeping euphemism is a sign of sickness in our system? One that allows us to accept a twisted logic that defines debt as valuable and where those who can least afford loans pay higher interest. Is the best explanation for this debt that global growth and prosperity are dependent on it, and that occasional adjustments and wobbles are necessary? All the time we use evasive terms we are really avoiding the human cost. Many people currently experiencing 'a correction' in this crisis are not reckless gamblers who shift debt or even lenders encouraging the taking of loans, but people simply trying to get by.

Maybe the system needs a different kind of correction, and a different kind of financial wisdom to the kind we've been buying these last few years: advice that doesn't use euphemism or hedge its bets, but that says what's at stake. If this sounds naïve it's been suggested before; take this from Exodus: 'iIf you lend money to one of my people among you who is needy... charge him no interest. If you take your neighbour's cloak as pledge give it back by sunset because his cloak is the only covering he has.' In this financial system lending isn't based on risk but on trust; its aim is for securing not exploiting, and people quite clearly come first before products.

24.9.2007

—

Christmas is always coming

Christmas is coming and there's nothing we can do to stop it. We know it's coming because the lights are already up, the trees are in, and because three doors on the advent calendar have been opened. We know it's coming because the prophets of anxiety are predicting a difficult time for the shoppers and retailers of our over-stretched, debt-ridden land. We feel the imminence of Christmas in the mincemeat sensations of excitement and dread; of wishing it would never end and wanting it over with now. Of the need to be at home – with family and friends – and the desire to escape it all and get as far away as possible.

As the Grinch in Dr Seuss' story says:

'Christmas! It's practically here!'

...Then he growled with his fingers nervously drumming,
'I must find a way to keep Christmas from coming!'

Advent means the arrival – or coming – of an important person or thing. Yet break it down into its compound words: 'ad' and 'vent' and it looks alarmingly like something to do with advertising and windows – it sounds like a big commercial wind. Which of course it is, has been, and probably always will be. Which is why Grinch-like, seasonal rants about the commercial aspect of Christmas will do nothing to change it.

Priests asking us not to throw out the baby Jesus with the bath salts should save their breath. If they want us to question anything at Christmas it should be the baby: Do we need the baby? Do we want the baby? What is this baby for? It's easy to see that Christmas 'doesn't come from a store'... easy to guess 'it means a little bit more'... the question for us all is: What?

Isaiah, a prophet who lived before Christ, framed our need in this way: 'O that you would tear open the heavens and come down.' There was an ache for a saviour long before one appeared. As to what this saviour is for, Isaiah put it in these startling terms: 'For those living in darkness, a light has come,' and later 'he will be pierced for our transgressions and by his wounds we are healed.'

For Isaiah it took 600 years and a thousand advent calendar windows before the double doors opened on the baby in the manger he predicted would be 'the saviour of the world.' That's a kind of patience – a kind of expectation and waiting – that's hard to grasp. In theory, for us, the waiting is over. The baby – whether we like it or not – is here – Immanuel or God with us. As the Grinch discovered, we can't stop Christmas from coming, 'Somehow or other, it came just the same!' The challenge for us this advent is finding the space to think about why it came at all in the first place.

3.12.2007

No more Christmas cards

One day, many years ago, we took a decision not to send Christmas cards. I forget the exact reasons for this, but I think it had something to do with a need to cut out tokenism; to somehow avoid the tyranny of obligation imposed by this festive season. Anyway, the experiment was a success because our tradition of not sending Christmas cards has stuck.

Naturally, there was a concern that a non-sending of cards would result in reciprocal action and for the first few years I could not stop myself from counting the cards on the walls and mantelpiece to see if people had noticed. While the numbers might have dropped off, the cards kept coming – which either proves that people don't read their Christmas cards carefully enough or that people are not so small minded as to stop sending you cards because you haven't sent them one. (That wouldn't be in the Christmas spirit, would it?)

So, for good or ill, we still get to see how much people's children have grown since we last saw them (on last year's Christmas cards); we still check to see if the card has a personal message other than the conveyor-belt seasonal greeting. Sometimes we are rewarded with a genuine message of love or of real information as opposed to the round-robin 'bulletins of brilliance' that accompany some cards; and yes, it is impossible not to feel, when looking at the well-strung line of cards bending down to the floor, that we are somehow loved and linked.

It's easy to sound curmudgeonly in all of this; a wise man surely accepts these superficial rituals as inevitable and 'part of it all'; a wise man knows that sending a message by post or internet is a way of being somewhere he can't be; and a wise man doesn't really assess his popularity by the number of Christmas cards he has. He knows that these cards are not a true reflection of his worth. He suspects that the number of cards he has – like the number of friends in a virtual network – is really a poor reflection of some greater reality, and some deeper need.

Christmas is, in part, about 'sending a message,' but it's more than a 'Hello, how are you?' asked every 12 months. Christmas is all about the tension between superficiality and depth, between absence and presence. The message of Christmas is that there is no substitute for being there – incarnate or, literally, in the flesh. No amount of words sent by post or by telephone or over social networking sites can ever match the visceral reality of presence. Face-to-phone or face-to-screen will never match face-to-face. Christmas is about face-to-face, about God stepping out of the virtual mainframe and into the reality of everyday relationships. It's about a God who stops sending us messages we don't really take seriously and becomes the message Himself.

17.12.2007

—

No country for middle-aged men

According to researchers at the University of Warwick, happiness over the course of our lives is u-shaped. For the average Briton, the mountain highs peak at the ages of 20 and 70, while the valley lows bottom out at 44. So, with my 44th birthday approaching, I am steeling myself for the year of living gloomily, contemplating the things that might have been, the tightening hamstrings, and the fact that I will probably never win an Oscar.

This is no country for middle-aged men.

We already have a name for what this data tells us, and it's called a mid-life crisis. That creeping, subconscious stocktake where the over-reaching ambitions we had in our twenties have been passed through the audit of our lives and found wanting; the credibility gap between our dreams and their realization yawns like an abyss. We've been cooking the books of our expectations and now our bodies, our bank balances, our lack of accolades are telling us we've reached our peak and, from where we stand, it's barely a hill.

Dante prefigures this moment in his *Inferno*: 'In the midway of this our mortal life, I found me in a gloomy wood, astray; Gone from the path direct.'

We sense we're not quite on track but we're not sure what to do about it. The parody panacea for this crisis is the sports car, the tuck or the youth – yearning athletic challenge. We do it even though we know – like Woody Allen watching the joggers overtake him in Central Park – that we are only 'staving off the inevitable.' If we don't medicate the crisis with stuff, we shift to a default position of grudging envy towards the blessed doubt-free – the beautiful people who win awards.

Yet according to the research, the joy dip in mid-life affects us all – rich, poor; famous, anonymous; saint or devil. In fact, the data suggests that unhappiness isn't attributable to a lack of material wealth or achievement. It even hints that the crisis could be an opportunity. An Aristotelian moment: the chance to examine the life and get our expectations and hopes in line with reality.

The writer of Ecclesiastes – the ultimate mid-life crisis manual – famously declared everything to be meaningless and that 'all is vanity'; but he didn't leave it there, languishing in a cool despair. He hints that we have been wired for something else: he suggests that God planted eternity in the hearts of men and that a life (or even half a life) lived in avoidance of this is what leads to a sense of pointlessness. True happiness has little to do with 'all things under the sun'; it lies in the unseen.

Behind much of the mid-life angst there lurks the need – the want – to be loved. You can hear it in the teary histrionics of an Oscar acceptance speech, and you can see it in the middle-aged man straining his body's abs to youthful flatness.

'Do you love me?' 'Will you remember me?' 'Will my life amount to something?' 'Am I a contender?' we ask. Perhaps the real question for someone half way through a life isn't 'How have I done?' or 'Have I measured up?' but 'Who is doing the measuring?'

26.2.2008

—

One wet Wednesday

I stumbled across Jesus three times yesterday. First, at the Royal Academy, Piccadilly, where he was hanging from a cross in a painting by the artist Lucas Cranach. He looked a little too fat to be Jesus, but the plinth said it was him. Then I saw him on the television, looking more like a good Jesus should and doing the things a good Jesus does. He said he'd rise again, and he didn't disappoint. Then he walked up an alleyway and disappeared. Finally, just before bedtime, I heard him – heard his words at any rate – on the radio. Some people were singing about him 'Being with us until the end of time.' Then I went to sleep.

When I woke up it was back to life; back to reality. They say that Jesus died on Good Friday and rose on Easter Sunday, but where is he now, on this wet Wednesday? The rumour that an image, a reflection, of the one true God has appeared within history has been dutifully accommodated by schedules and programmes. Now, maybe it's time to put the rumour back in its box – or tomb – and leave it there for another year. Jesus has got his column inches. We need to get back to the things that are more relevant to our lives; and back to the stories that are rooted in *this* world.

Three days after Easter there are plenty of these. Stories such as the brave protestors in Tibet taking on a mighty empire at the risk of sacrificing their own lives; the oppressed voters of Zimbabwe facing intimidation for putting a simple cross on a ballot paper; or the mother of the 4,000th American soldier to die in Iraq, weeping at the loss of her only son. This is real news. What does Jesus have to do with any of this?

For some reason the rumour of his immanence won't go away. It doesn't stay neatly fixed to a date in a moon-made calendar. It seems to have a mysterious life of its own; it sneaks into conversations. It pops up not just in art galleries and television dramas, but apparently in people's lives. If Jesus is to be believed, it is through these lives that he can be found transforming the bad news of the world into good.

'Why do you look for me among the dead?' Jesus asked. Before directing us to look for him among the living. It might be in the streets of Lhasa, Baghdad and Harare – among the oppressed, the mourners and the hungry. Or wherever one or two are gathered – in a car, a kitchen or an office. Or we may just encounter him among ordinary, everyday people; the kind of people that listen to the news, as well as those who make it. Even those who have tuned in on a wet Wednesday morning in March, 2008, Anno Domini.

26.3.2008

—

The $50,000 loaf

My daughter has a collection of foreign currency in a string purse. Her favourite is a pink, $50,000 note from Zimbabwe that she picked up from our visit there two years ago. The notes were printed in order to accommodate the inflation that then stood at 1,000 per cent. At the time, $50,000 was enough to buy a loaf of bread.

Now, I hope she'll get to keep this note, not as a momento of dark times, but as a sign that things can change. With the Zimbabwe election results hanging in the balance, could it be that this destructive escalation is finally coming to an end; that the leadership that has overseen Zimbabwe's descent from Africa's breadbasket to basket case is about to step down? The wait is unbearable but, as Morgan Tsvangiri – potentially the new president of Zimbabwe – said last night: 'The people have been waiting this long, they can wait a little longer.'

For those of us blessed with free choice, opinion and daily bread, it is hard to understand how a people could have put up with this for so long. When we were there two years ago conditions were so bad it seemed extraordinary that the people were still tolerating the leadership. We kept thinking something had to give; that there would be some Berlin-wall style uprising to force the change that previous elections had failed to deliver. Yet there was only a strange, listless tension. The people were either supernaturally patient or just afraid.

After a few conversations the reality became clear: they were worn out. A living example of the Psalmist's lament: 'While the wicked live on, growing old and increasing in power, the people groan.' They may have wanted to rise up, but they seemed too tired to do it. Their day's greatest challenge was simply trying to get enough money to buy bread.

The question I kept asking people was, 'How have you survived?' The answer I got from some taxi drivers was this: 'We are hoping that things will get better one day. God will see us through. Things will change.' When I asked them if they really believed this they said, 'Hope is all we have. It's what keeps us going.' I felt chastized. For them hope was as sustaining as bread, a currency with a dependable rate.

Today, as we watch the Zimbabwean people waiting – again with almost supernatural patience – we can see the value of this kind of hope: a worn out, underfed, double-duped people, have actually gone to the polls and put faith in a system that has let them down in the past. They know they might see their hopes dashed again, but they have gone to vote because they still believe it might change things. So, as they wait, let's wait with them, hoping that they get what they have asked for. Someone who will give them freedom and bread at a price they can afford.

2.4.2008

What people want to hear

In elections across the world, it seems voters are having to develop supernatural levels of insight in order to choose the right person for a particular office. Not because politicians are suddenly of a lower standard than ever before; but because in a world of carefully tailored messages, it's becoming harder to know what a person really stands for based on what they say.

In America, for instance, Hilary Clinton says she would not hesitate to give the order to press the button that obliterates a nation of 40 million people. It's hard not to hear in this someone who knows that talking tough on Iran also presses the buttons of the people whose votes she needs. Even Barrack Obama's strong denunciation of his former pastor Jeremiah Wright's preaching seems to have one eye on the offended sensibilities of the people who might vote for him next time.

This is an age-old problem for politicians – good and bad – constantly having to check their words; negotiating a complex balance between saying what they think and what *they* think most people want to hear. It is possible and it should be possible for politicians to say what they believe and for us to believe them, but it says something that, even in democracies where people are free to say what they want, some still seem afraid to do so.

If so, this is a spiritual as well as political problem. We end up creating a system that favours people-pleasers who say things they don't really mean in order to gain power over those who really have something to say and mean it. A kind of, he who flatters wins situation. Such a system ends up diluting substance and feeding us soundbites and presentation. By the time the words are filtered via the media, the gap between appearance and reality is often so distorted it's hard to discern what is true.

Woodie Guthrie once wrote a song with the lyric, 'Jesus Christ For President', but I doubt Jesus would fare any better at the hustings. It's said he didn't look great; he often said provocative things to the wrong people at exactly the wrong time; he hung out with people of little consequence, delivered a very off-putting and baffling manifesto, and had a kind of anti-spin approach to public relations. His campaign ended not in election to high office, but in death.

Yet the man who turned down the offer of earthly power and who was despised and rejected by many, seems to have got his message through. He has more followers than any head of state. Millions of people can still quote his manifesto today and some even try and implement his policies. Jesus once said, 'Woe to you when all men think well of you.' Good advice perhaps for those politicians seeking popularity at the expense of character, power at the price of principle. Maybe if you want your message to stick, say what you believe, but don't expect people to love you for it.

1.5.2008

—

A religious experience

This week I was at an outdoor rock concert, something that's now as sure a fixture on the summer calendar as Wimbledon or a bank holiday. Half way through a beautiful song by the band Radiohead my friend, who as far as I know has no religious affiliations, turned to me with tears in his eyes and said that he was having a religious experience. He wasn't being glib. Something was happening in that moment; something powerful enough to make him cry, embrace me and for both of us raise our hands in a gesture of abandoned praise. We both knew, without saying so, that we weren't worshipping the band – great though they are – and that this 'something' was about more than just music; but what was it?

Of course, I can I explain it all rationally: the sonic vibrations coursing down the cerebral cortex, the mass gathering of people and the quantity of beer were all combining to produce a heightened feeling of euphoria. Yet should I write off what my friend was saying purely on the grounds of it being just a feeling? I think he was experiencing something that many of us do, but can't always name – that sense of something beyond ourselves and the feeling of rapture and exaltation that goes with it. The music – like stunning scenery or a fine painting – was really just a window through which he caught a glimpse of 'the other', the something beyond the veil of what we can see with our eyes and explain with our minds.

As the apostle Paul – a man who had a spectacular 3D religious experience – once put it: 'Since the creation of the world God's invisible qualities can been clearly seen all around us.' In all that is beautiful and excellent, in all that is good, creation shouts and whispers the rumour of the divine.

I think those tears at the rock concert were a response to the same force of divine Love that revealed itself to Paul; but I also think there's more. The theologian Rudolf Otto – who called this sense of 'the tremendous' or the mysterious – 'the numinous' – also said that a religious experience required an ethical dimension. Implying that the full measure of the religious experience was not how spectacular it was – but the fruit it bore. A special effect needs to have a special effect.

When the prophet Isaiah had his fantastic encounter with God his response wasn't so much 'Wow!', but woe: 'Woe to me for I am a man of unclean lips,' he said. It's this response rather than the seraphim or the blinding light figure on the throne that makes it meaningful. The experience lead to an instant inner transformation. Interestingly, Isaiah doesn't go and tell people about the vision. He tells them to turn to God, to help the sick and the poor and broken. Or as Paul himself bluntly put it: if you really want a religions experience, go and look after the widows and the orphans.

27.6.2008

Heart murmur

I recently went to have my heart checked out for a life assurance policy. As I drove to the hospital, I found myself worrying. Anxieties about my health, about my finances and about my mortality were being stirred up in one big cocktail of concern. What if they discover some defect? What if they refuse the cover? What if they find out that I'm about to die? As the nurse pressed the jellied metal plate to my back, I imagined the ultrasound detecting my innermost fears or suddenly telling me how long I had to live. I tried to calm down: my anxiety was surely increasing the chances of something bad being picked up.

'Relax and breathe normally,' the nurse said, before flipping a switch that enabled me to hear the amplified pumping of my heart valves. At first, the sound of my life-blood coursing through me was disconcerting. Was my whole earthly existence really dependent on this mulchy squelch? It all sounded so fragile. After a few minutes, an oddly calming thought came to me: this heart of mine had been getting on with its job for 44 years with little help from me. With that I began to relax and feel grateful for the life this miraculous pump had given me (not to mention the free treatment I was receiving from the NHS. Thank God for every one of its 60 years!).

Right now, the irregular beats of the global economy are causing sharp pains for many people. A great stethoscope has been pressed to the heart of the world and picked up an alarming number of complications. In housing, in food, in petrol, things aren't as healthy as we thought, but the diagnosis is important, maybe even life-saving. The economic insecurity reminds us of something we all already know but prefer to let lie beneath the surface: namely that we're not as in control of our lives as we think and that to cling to this illusion is unhealthy – even deadly.

Jesus's counsel to the worried wasn't 'Next time make better plans', but 'Trust God for your daily needs and let not your heart be troubled. Don't worry about tomorrow because today has enough trouble of its own.' This command not to fret (and it is a command and not a suggestion) is not a piece of careful commonsense, but a statement about reality: we can't control the future, but we can live fully in the present.

At its heart lies a vital question: what – or who – do we think is in control of our lives? Ourselves? The doctors? The banks? Can God look after the small detail of our lives – or do we take on the burden of worry ourselves? We can choose to fear or we can choose to hope, but the choice is always a heart issue, because the heart is the repository of both.

5.7.2008

—

The law of love

While talking over some of this week's news stories with a good friend, he concluded that we were now living in a society where people were too afraid to speak out about what was right and what was wrong. In his view, a healthy society needed clear notions of morality, but a creeping relativism was leading us into trouble. I nodded in partial agreement, but I couldn't stop myself from hearing in these words the ghosts of past 'back to basics' lessons and 'family values' lectures. A reaction that often seems to arise in the aftermath of an appalling crime that exposes – what is often quoted as – 'the moral drift of society'.

When my friend moved from the general to the particular, we began to get to the heart of the issue. He said that he'd had a strict moral upbringing from parents who had clear beliefs about what was good and what was bad, but admitted that while the rules they'd given him had kept him on track, the living out of those rules was hard. He knew 'in his head' what he shouldn't do, but as he got older the boundaries felt more like barriers. The feelings of restriction created resentment rather than reformation. In the end, he rebelled.

His honest confession raised a serious question: namely that you can try and legislate for morality – but how do you teach it? How do we get the knowledge of what is right and wrong to go from our heads to our hearts and hence to the practice of our lives? Even my own children – whom I parent with an alarming mixture of liberal abandon punctuated by sporadic bouts of snapped reactionary regulation – can spot the difference between me telling them what not to do and me actually helping them not to do it. The difference, if you like, between bad disciplining and good discipling. If I am being honest, I tend to default to the former (the laying down of the law) because the latter (teaching by example) is too much like hard work. It takes time, effort and commitment to teach right from wrong – in short, it takes love.

Jesus (who said he had come to fulfil the law, not do away with it) sums it up this way when he tells us to obey the 'don't do' commandments, but to understand that these laws are summarized by the one great law that is defined and experienced through loving God and our neighbour. He really gives us a statement of what the purpose of morality is: it isn't about living a meagre life of restriction and constraint, telling people what to eat or what to not to do; it's about living life to the full and helping others to become or to grow or to change into people who can do the same. Yes, we need the law, but if we want to live abundantly, it must be the law of love.

12.7.2008

—

The big question

Instead of going to church this Sunday I went with my family to the Natural History Museum. If we weren't formally going to worship God, then maybe we could – like the Psalmist – worship him by admiring his handiwork. Given that the museum's mission statement is 'To inspire awe and wonder', perhaps the two things would join up.

As we entered the cathedral-like structure we joined other seekers on a walk through the universe. We saw how stars and planets were formed, how the earth was shaped, how life began, and we began to feel the thrill of facts and mystery aligning and colliding in our minds and souls. It was hard not to feel awe for the universe we inhabit and wonder at our place in it. Impossible to ignore the curling of the big question: how did we get here?

Then (as if strategically placed to supply the answer) we walked towards the Darwin exhibition, where a poster depicted the superabundantly hirsute biologist raising a shushing finger to his mouth. The line on the poster asked: 'If you had an idea that was going to outrage society, would you keep it to yourself?'

We now know that Darwin's great idea (that life evolves from one family tree) did outrage society. Not least, because it seemed to imply to some that there was no need for a Creator. While many believers tried to understand the implications of Darwin's idea for their faith, a high profile and noisy face-off mutated the scientific theory into a theological debate that polarized the argument. Like the leap between two species, the schism looked eternally unbridgeable.

Darwin saw the polarization as a false one, declaring it 'absurd to doubt that a man could be an ardent Theist and an evolutionist.' Towards the end of his life – possibly exasperated at the extreme responses his theory had evoked – Darwin wrote to his friend, the vicar John Innes: 'I hardly see how religion and science can be kept distinct, but I most wholly agree with you that there is no reason why the disciples of either school should attack each other with bitterness.'

Today – with the theory evolved into fact – there is more reverence than outrage for Darwin's idea. Yet there are some who refuse to accept it for fear that it undermines their own beliefs. Sir David Attenborough still receives hate mail for failing to credit God in his documentaries about life on Earth. I'm not sure which is worse: a national treasure getting vitriol from people who profess to believe in a loving God, or a people failing to engage with an idea for fear that it may challenge them.

As we left the museum my son said he didn't understand why people couldn't believe in a God and the theory of evolution. He said he was 'cool with both' and I'd like to think that God and Darwin would agree with him. For Truth is surely the heaven that faith and science are both seeking. Perhaps awe and wonder are the things that join them on that journey.

29.1.2009

—

Snow sermon

Most Sunday evenings I sit down with my wife and go over what's going to happen in the week. It's a helpful exercise: it prepares us for what's coming and gives us the temporary illusion of being in control of our lives. Like millions of other people I went to bed on Sunday with a pretty clear idea of how the week was going to pan out. In my case, it would start with me getting on a plane and going to a meeting that I thought was important.

Yet when I woke it didn't sound as if anything was happening. There were no planes flying overhead or cars passing by. A still, numinous silence emanated from the seven-o'clock street. Ripping back the curtains my daughter clarified the situation: 'Look Dad, snow! Really deep, heavy snow!' Her observation was followed by the confident announcement that there would be no school that day – and probably no work – and that this was going to be fun.

Sure enough, a few hours later, instead of finding myself in a meeting being totally serious about my life, I found myself rolling snowballs in the park with a bunch of children, the deputy head of a local school and an IT manager, along with hundreds of completely snowbound strangers. Instead of stopping to ask if this was sensible or productive use of our time, we used our mitts to make a giant snowball and our wits to calculate how much it weighed. It was hard to discern who the grown-ups were.

This week, Britain's biggest snow dump in 18 years has turned a lot of adults into children and many a weekly plan to mulch. This being British snow, the moment melted quickly and the madcap fun soon froze into icy recriminations about health and safety, shut schools and the cost of it all. I don't want to belittle these things, and it's a sad fact that the snow has claimed lives this week, but for just a couple of days, the massive fall did something that most religions struggle to do.

No respecter of rank or importance, the snow is a great leveller; it settles on teachers and pupils without discrimination. It mocks the self-important and trips up the well sorted, it forces people to notice things around them – like other people; and it maybe gets them to consider something bigger than themselves. Even the author of the book of Job (who can't have seen much of the white stuff) once wrote: 'God's voice thunders in marvellous ways. He says to the snow: Fall on the earth. He stops every man from his labour, so that all men may know his work.'

This week the snow delivered a beautiful sermon on the importance of being – not doing. It pointed out that an activity doesn't have to have a discernible economic benefit to be valid. It showed us that adults need to be like children and taught children things they're not necessarily going to learn in school. Including the fact that a snowball two meters in diameter and half the density of water weighs just over two tons.

Just because something's heavy and deep, it doesn't mean it can't be fun.

5.2.2009

A pig in lipstick

Until this week I'd never heard this expression that a pig in lipstick is still just a pig, but ever since Barack Obama dropped his porcine phrase two days ago, I can't get the image of hogs in Revlon out of my head. It's unsettling. Kind of like *Animal Farm* meets *Moulin Rouge*.

It turns out this aphorism – which essentially means trying to dress something up to look like it isn't – is well known in America and has been used before, notably by John McCain when describing Hilary Clinton's policies. The problem for Obama wasn't the phrase but the timing. Only last week McCain's choice for Vice President, Sarah Palin, used a cosmetic quip when she described herself as a pit-bull in lipstick. Whether Obama meant it or not, it was hard not to hear him calling Palin something he shouldn't and for some people to conclude that he was, perhaps, being a male chauvinist pig.

The slip may be forgiven, but it's a reminder that words matter. The wrong word or phrase spoken at the wrong moment can undo a man. In the case of politicians, it can break their election prospects. Although we'd like to think that substance not cosmetics is what the electorate is looking for, it's often words, or a choice phrase like Bill Clinton's 'It's the economy stupid', that decide it.

The pig phrase actually has an equivalent in a proverb that says, 'A gold ring in a pig's nose is like a fair woman who lacks discretion.' Yet discretion – or not speaking when you want to – is a hard thing to find in a world that demands an instant, preferably shiny, response. Short pauses – or 'pig's whispers' as they are known – are often regarded with suspicion, even confusion. I remember the Archbishop of Canterbury, being interviewed, taking ten seconds before answering a question because he wanted to consider his words rather than give a glib, air-wave filling response. Those ten seconds of not saying anything were about the most eloquent thing I've heard on the radio.

The scriptures take words and their effects, both positive and negative, very seriously. The tongue can speak life if it chooses; but it can also curse, slander and kill. Which is why, as another proverb tells us, holding it can keep us from calamity. Like a small rudder on a big boat, the tongue can very quickly steer us on a course we never intended to take. It's interesting that Jesus chose not to use any words just at the point when they might have saved him.

In Paul's letter to the Romans there's this extraordinary and sobering statement that one day we will all have to account for every word we've ever uttered. No wonder that the prophet Isaiah's instant response upon encountering God was to say 'woe to me for I am a man of unclean lips' and then to say absolutely nothing for several days. The holy man knew he'd said things that were ugly, and no amount of lipstick could hide the fact.

11.2.2009

—

Golden bulls

Whether it's a pickled calf in formaldehyde at Sotheby's or a snorting bronze statue outside the investment bank, Merrill Lynch, it's been a big week for bulls. With potent timing the biggest art sale by a single artist in history has coincided with the biggest bank collapse in one hundred years. It's hard to work out if it's exquisitely apt or crassly coincidental that the centrepiece of the Damien Hirst auction was a dead bull with 18-carat hooves and horns entitled 'The Golden Calf'.

This piece, which fetched a record £10.2 million, may have sent Hirst laughing all the way to a bank somewhere that isn't collapsing, but his works – and the money paid for them – have provoked real ire from the high priests of the art world – most notably Robert Hughes, who has, like some latter day Moses, come down from the mountain where the true gods of art are worshipped, to pulverize the false idol and make its worshippers eat its meaningless dust.

On the money thing, I'm with Hirst who in his defence recites the world's first immutable commandment: 'Thou shalt determine the worth of a thing by what a man is willing to pay.' On the art thing, it's surely a matter of taste. Personally, I think his work is a perfect document for years of bull markets, sharks in financial institutions, butterfly schemes and dotty spending. Although my idolatory will forever be checked by my son who, upon being taken to see the famous shark, asked me if the artist had caught it himself.

More seriously, Hirst's work reminds us of our collective ability to go for something quick, easy and accessible over something difficult, that perhaps requires a lifetime's blood, sweat and patience. The artist seems smart enough to know this. He even included a note with the drawings of the Golden Calf warning its purchaser 'not to go worshipping false idols'.

Some might say it's too late for that, but I think we all have our golden calves; things that are not worthy of our worship, but that we bow down to anyway. Like the Israelites who got bored of waiting for Moses to finish talking to the invisible God, we all have a tendency to go for gods we can feel, touch and see rather than one who expects people to wait and trust him for something better.

The prophet Isaiah actually has God putting it this way: 'To whom will you compare me? Some pour out gold; hire a goldsmith and make a god. They set it in its place and there it stands; but when someone cries out to it, it doesn't answer.' Perhaps, when the loud, shiny gods of this world have been found wanting, it's time to look beyond the obvious and re-consider the true value of the invisible.

19.2.2009

—

God must really love you!

Not long ago, a friend of mine who lives in a village in Kenya came to stay. When she walked into our house she looked around and started to chuckle. Then, without a hint of envy she said: 'God must really love you.'

Now I'm grateful for every square foot I live in and am not embarrassed to thank God for it, but this observation made me feel uneasy. It wasn't just the idea of there being a correlation between God's love and the size of someone's real estate; or the relative scale of my house compared to my friend's hut back in Kenya. No, it was the subtler, murkier truth that it was a bank that had helped provide this blessing – and it was a blessing that came with conditions.

Later, as I showed her around the streets where I live, I attempted to disabuse her of the idea that all these houses equated to riches. When I said that most people took on big debts to live in their homes and owed more money than any of her fellow Kenyans she looked incredulous. They may not have had street lighting or running water in her village, but everyone owned their home. How, she asked, could people in such a rich country have such debts?

Her question echoed in my mind this week as the chancellor announced a national debt of £1.4 trillion; a debt that will amount to 79 per cent of GDP by 2013. A figure incidentally that's 10 per cent worse than Kenya's – a supposed third world debtor nation. In fact, you don't hear the phrase third world debt much these days; it's been drowned out by the trillion pound tsunami of first world debt we've been surfing for the last decade.

How *did* we get here? Well, in part, because debt has become the accepted and necessary condition for economic activity – the means by which we can live our lives to a standard we expect. Without borrowing, most people can't afford a house, a car or further education. Although we have a sense that debt isn't ideal, we have disguised its more toxic effects through the use of euphemisms like gearing or leverage, re-packaging debt as a good thing.

It is often said that our culture and laws have been shaped by the wisdom of Judeo-Christian principles, but we have been highly selective about which bits we heed, ignoring the advice that doesn't fit our way of life. Thus, the proverb that 'a borrower is made slave to a lender' is said to belong to another age. We thank God for a mortgage lending rate of 3.2 per cent per annum while ignoring the words that say, 'Money lent at interest leads to destruction.'

Those same scriptures actually suggest we should have no debt to anyone except the debt to love one another, and that God's blessing never has conditions attached – something my Kenyan friend genuinely believed. I don't want to idealize the lives of people who live in a country that can't even tarmac its main roads or provide free secondary education, but I can't get away from the fact that my friend is richer than me – not because she *owns* a lot, but because she *owes* nothing.

24.4.2009

—

What is essential?

This week I received a text message from a friend who lives in a rural town in Kenya. The text read: 'Merry Xmas. May your family be blessed with what is truly essential.' I was about to reply in kind when I hesitated. Not because I didn't want to bless him back, but because I wasn't sure if it would mean the same thing. After all, he lives in a town where what is essential means having enough beans to get through the drought; I live in a town where (even in recession) people can serve three types of cream with the Christmas pudding and still feel aggrieved at having to cancel a skiing holiday. I doubted that my response to him was going to represent a fair exchange of blessing.

His phrase 'what is essential' hung around my slightly mulled head all day. Even in these tightening times, did I even know what essential looked like? Would I – in order to learn its true meaning – have to do without all the stuff that I was currently enjoying – like a holiday and movies and wine? It didn't help that in the midst of my bloated Christmas this message had come from a man in a town without running water.

Some people, particularly church leaders, are suggesting that this current economic crisis might help focus our minds on what matters. People will buy what they need instead of what they want; and will learn to be grateful for having what much of the world doesn't: sufficient food, clean water and rooves over their heads. Yet appreciating what is essential surely takes more than being frugal or being thankful that you're better off than most people in the world (and even the harshest correction to our economy won't take us anywhere near to evening out that difference).

The author of *The Little Prince*, St Exupery, once wrote, 'What is essential is invisible.' He was echoing the apostle Paul who wrote that the things we see are transient; but the things we do not see are eternal. If you think this is so much fairytale philosophy, write a list of ten things you think essential. When I wrote my list only two of the things – work and health – were visible; the rest (which included love, hope, freedom and God) were all unseen, immeasurable and imperishable.

Perhaps if we are to understand what is essential, we must become people who invest in things that don't fall apart – or as Jesus put it: 'Provide purses for yourselves that will not wear out, a treasure in heaven that will not be exhausted.' This might involve a stripping away of what is unimportant, but it's not about choosing a reductive economic ascetic; it's about gaining true riches.

Guilty meditation over, I finally got over myself and sent back the message to my friend hoping that he too would be blessed with the essentials; yes, things even more important than water, food or clothes. When all is stripped away, what is essential to a person in Kenya is essential to a person in Britain.

May you too be blessed with what is essential in the coming year.

30.5.2009

—

Fiona and Francesca

Seeing the faces of Fiona Pilkington and her daughter Francesca on the news and listening to the newsreader outlining the facts from the inquest into their deaths, I found myself wishing he'd move quickly on to something else – the missile launch in Iran, or the sleazy drama of Polanski's arrest or even the peculiar rhetoric of a political party conference. Some news stories are so painful you just don't want to know the details.

I wanted to put this tragic tale of two unsung and vulnerable people in that category of events that illustrate a wider malaise in our country – one of those social tragedies from the front line of what some like to call 'Broken Britain.' I'd lazily blame the police, the social services and those anti-social kids and move on – to other news. Yet this story doesn't really allow for such dismissive explanations. It's more complex and it's too close to home. Maybe this is what makes it so difficult to face.

While the observable facts suggest a collective failure – of the police to protect the vulnerable, of the social services to communicate; and even of the local community to anticipate what was about to happen – none of these things fully explain the despair that led to a woman taking her own life and that of her daughter. At the conference yesterday, the government promised to 'fight anti-social behaviour wherever it is'; but as Fiona Pilkington's own parish priest suggested, we can't just put our community life in the hands of outside agencies. We have to take some responsibility ourselves.

My own discomfort with this story lies partly in seeing myself in the shoes of the abusers as well as those of the neighbours. I was once in a group of boys that was paid in Mars Bars to verbally abuse an older pupil to the point of breakdown. We weren't socially deprived, or even bored. We were just cruel and thoughtless. Even to this day, through busyness or self-interest, I choose to ignore the needs of my neighbours. Only last week I crossed the road to avoid saying hello to a man I knew had some personal difficulties simply because I didn't want the hassle.

The day before Fiona and Francesca died their neighbour took a Bakewell Tart round to their house. In a heart rending interview she expressed what probably no politician, policeman or church minister could say, namely that if she had known what was going to happen she would have stayed with them – all through the night if that's what it took.

Hopefully this sad story will lead to some changes in the way our society protects its most vulnerable, but we should remember that we too can be agents of the very things that can save a neighbour from despair. As it says in Romans, 'We who are strong ought to bear with the failings of the weak and not please ourselves. Each of us should please his neighbour for their good, to build them up – for even Christ did not please himself but, as it is written, 'The insults of those who insult you have fallen on me.'

30.9.2009

—

School of faith

This week, the UK's new supreme court is debating whether parents should have to prove an adequate level of religious observance in order to get their children into a faith school. At the heart of the debate lie some key questions: What is an adequate level of religious observance? Is faith a matter of who you are – or what you do? Can you even measure it?

The criteria for entry into most Christian faith schools involve some proof of church attendance, baptism or confirmation and maybe a letter of recommendation from the church leader. As anyone who lives within the catchment area of a faith school knows, there are plenty of parents willing to sit through Sundays of strange and sometimes tedious ritual in order to give their child a decent education. As John Wazcek, the headmaster of a Catholic school in Liverpool, recently said: 'Who is to say that someone who runs a football club on a Sunday isn't being a better Christian than someone who regularly attends church?'

Ironically, it's hard to imagine Jesus himself endorsing a system that asks parents to jump through a series of ritual hoops, when so much of what he said blows apart the cultural, ethnic and geographical conditions of entry that the religious authorities insisted on. If we can't define faith by where someone lives, what their parents believe, or how often they attend a particular meeting in a building – how can we define it?

Jesus once gave an answer to this question when he met with a great teacher called Nicodemus who, as a member of the religious ruling council, would have known all about the schooling of faith. Nicodemus began by calling Jesus a teacher who had surely come from God – but Jesus cut to the chase: insulting Nicodemus' piety by saying 'No one can see the Kingdom of God without being born again.' The criteria for entry into *his* 'faith school' was not family, ethnicity or nationality – or even the outward signs of religious observance – but a total revolution within the spirit of that person; a revolution that re-directs allegiance away from who you are or what you do – to who you follow.

I imagine that if faith schools really were committed to following the teachings of Jesus then the problem of over-subscription or who gets in and who doesn't would be solved in an instant; for perhaps not many parents would send their kids to a school that insisted on you being born again, or its pupils putting their allegiance to Jesus above their parents; or that asked parents when they last fed the poor and if they were willing to sell everything they had to get in?

In the end most parents just want a good education for their children. However, we need to be clear and honest about the fact that any schooling system that selects on academic, economic or faith grounds is by definition exclusive; and that such exclusivity really has no place in the 'school of faith' Jesus established.

29.10.2009

—

Laptop in the bath

I knew I had a problem when I found myself attempting to read my emails on my laptop while sitting in the bath. I'd even filled the tub with my wife's pine oils so that I could enjoy a moment of relaxation, and yet I just couldn't stop myself from balancing the computer over the bubbles and checking those messages. The next day my addiction was confirmed by my daughter who, when I offered to listen to her reading said, 'What's the use, Dad? You'll still do your emails at the same time.'

It seems I'm not alone in my struggle to keep the necessary but addictive traits of communication technology from becoming a tyranny. Over half of us spend more time with our computers than our spouses; while researchers at Loughborough University have found that an office worker works an average of three minutes before being interrupted by email – and that it takes them 64 seconds to recover their train of thought after that. That's a lot of people struggling to think straight.

The technology adds a lot to life and I'm not sure I could do my work without it; but there are times when I feel the constant access creates a kind of restless, electronic fidgeting – and a dependency that not only eats up the mental attention and makes intellectual focus hard; but that blurs the distinction between rest and work leaving me unrelaxed, tetchy and actually less likely to communicate well.

When Samuel Morse sent the first 'electronic message' in 1844 with the words: 'What hath God wrought?' he was already anticipating that newer and quicker forms of communicating would be both a blessing and a curse. The challenge for us – with technology about to unleash a platform that will allow us to simultaneously twitter, phone and email – isn't so much to put up a Luddite resistance as to ask, 'How we can best live with this stuff?'

There's no question that we're creatures wired for communication, but it can't just be about speed and immediacy – or even about words. Indeed, the monastic traditions saw self-control, listening and not speaking as essential for the kind of deep communication some believe we were created for. 'Be still and know that I am God' – the Psalmist wrote or, to paraphrase: 'Switch off, dial down and tune into another kind of communication – the kind that allows the mind the experience of a deeper, uninterrupted level of thought – where creativity and complex thinking can happen and where we may even hear a different voice.'

I once tried an experiment just before starting work of sitting in a chair for half an hour without doing anything, thinking anything or trying to communicate with anyone. It's an exquisitely difficult exercise and one I failed badly. Yet before I drop my laptop in the bath or ignore my daughter again, I'm going to give it another try and maybe, with God's help, I'll be able to sit there not sending messages – until I get the message.

5.11.2009

Money through the door

A few years ago, when I was out of work and struggling to pay the rent, a hand-delivered, brown envelope came through my front door. It contained a thousand pounds in cash and no explanatory note. As if that weren't amazing enough, it was almost exactly the amount I needed to pay my landlord. The anonymity of the giver left me with no one to thank but God – which was, I suspect, partly the point of the gift.

Watching the winners of Britain's biggest ever lottery haul receive their cheques this week, I found myself wondering who or what they would thank for the millions they had randomly won. For when that kind of money unexpectedly comes your way it feels like someone, somewhere needs to be thanked. Would it be God, Lady Luck, Camelot or the computer that selected their numbers? In the end, most seemed to favour a confusing syndicate of all four.

As it seems so unsatisfactory attributing such huge winnings to blind luck, it's not unusual for us to fill the void by constructing narratives explaining why particular people have won; stories that claim they somehow deserved it because of a humble background or difficult circumstances or because of the good things they intended to spend the money on. Anything but admit that lottery money is essentially money for nothing that doesn't come through love, kindness, hard work or generosity.

Despite money going to good causes, the lottery almost certainly transgresses the first, eighth and tenth commandments; it encourages people to put their hopes in the god of chance; gamble, and perhaps covet the fancy camels and chariots the winners will inevitably buy with their new found money. Behind all these commandments lies the issue of who or what we put our hope and trust in. While lots were drawn in biblical times, they were always a means of determining the will of God and underpinned by a belief that nothing in the universe is down to chance.

The faces of lottery winners are a compelling sight, caught as they are in a life-changing moment, they are people experiencing an unmerited favour – a kind of grace that must be close to being a religious experience. Yet for me it's still a favour bereft of any real meaningful, relational connection – and a pale imitation of the amazing grace that scripture describes. For the source of this grace isn't a faceless, magical tombola distributing money to the few, but a God who whose grace is intended to make us all rich.

Whatever force lay behind the pushing of £1,000 through my letterbox, my guess is it wasn't prompted by the chance tumbling of numbers in a machine, but by a considered act of kindness. I didn't deserve it and I still don't know who gave it to me, but it must have come from someone who knew me, cared about the detail of my life, didn't expect my thanks and believed that it's love not money that makes the world go round.

12.11.2009

—

Hypocrite!

There's a story in the Bible that always terrified me. It appears in the book of Acts and tells of a couple called Ananias and Sapphira. They were part of a church filled with people living remarkably generous and transparent lives. This couple had seemingly done a good thing, selling a piece of property and donating the proceeds to the church community. In an attempt to appear more generous, more spiritual, than they were, they acted as if they were donating all the proceeds. When the apostle Peter discovered this, both husband and wife were struck down dead. For years I mistakenly thought this was a story about the perils of not giving enough. Then I realized, it wasn't the money that led to their destruction – it was the hypocrisy.

I found myself thinking of this while hearing the news about Northern Island's first minister, Peter Robinson, and his wife Iris' affair and alleged financial impropriety. This tale is freighted with enough elements of scandal – sex, money and politics – to fuel a thousand column inches of comment. While the messy intersection of the public and the private may justify it as a scandal that matters, it's a perceived moral hypocrisy in the protagonists that's generated the most words and the toughest judgements.

Hypocrisy means 'putting on a mask.' Jesus coined the word, borrowing it from the Greek actors, or hypocrites, who entertained crowds at the outdoor theatres where he lived. It describes a person who puts on a face to make a good impression. While He knew it was something we're all capable of, He was quick to point it out in the lives of those who had power and responsibility – especially those in religious authority: 'Be on your guard against the yeast of the Pharisees, which is hypocrisy…' He said. 'Do not do what they do, for they do not practice what they preach.'

I think that story of Ananias and Sapphira scared me because deep down I know I've often said one thing and done another – or masked the inner reality of my feelings with an outward appearance that conveys the opposite. Yes, the consequences of hypocrisy are magnified in the lives of public figures, but it's a mode of being we can all adopt. Novelist Somerset Maugham wrote, 'Hypocrisy is the most difficult and nerve-racking vice any man can pursue; it needs an unceasing vigilance and a rare detachment of spirit. It cannot, like adultery or gluttony, be practiced at spare moments; it is a full-time job.'

It doesn't need to end there. There's an alternative to hypocrisy, and that's honesty. This doesn't mean attempting to be perfect – that only leads to legalism and pride. Better to pull off the masks, even if it involves a painful ripping away, and risk being seen by all for who we really are. If we are 'true to ourselves' it opens a door to grace that covers a multitude of transgressions. If hypocrisy is a barrier to receiving this grace, honesty keeps the road to life open.

12.1.2010

Leaders will fail

You can never say how long it will take, but as sure as gravity keeps our feet on the ground, it will happen. Sooner or later, people grow disappointed with their leaders. Yes, even a leader like Barack Obama who, a year ago today, looked to some like a one-man, world-righting phenomena, but whose mantra is now turning from a 'yes we can' to a 'well, maybe we can't just yet.' His approval ratings have dropped from 75 per cent to 53 per cent, the lowest of any president a year into office.

If these figures represent change that's hard to believe in, they probably tell us more about people's expectations than the failure of leaders. Rarely has a man been freighted with such unreasonable hope as President Obama. To be fair, he was smart enough to address this from day one; while the people jumped up and down and hollered their support, his measured words signalled an awareness that he was probably going to let them down in some way.

I'm not saying we shouldn't have high expectations of leaders or do what the financier Bernard Baruch advised and 'vote for the man who promises least because he'll be the least disappointing.' Yet disappointment with leaders is so universal, it's probably wise to recalibrate our expectations of them – maybe install a warning light that goes on whenever we start putting our hopes on the back of one person?

The tendency to look for a saviour is hard to curb. People want a superhero. From football to presidents, they are looking for the special one who's going to change everything, which is why it's helpful to be reminded that leaders are just people. I found it a relief when President Obama fluffed his lines at his inaugural address. It's only when a man stops being a superhero that people start thinking: 'Hang on. I want you to lead, but you can't save the world on your own and nor should you try.'

In the book of Samuel, when the people of Israel – fed up with a lack of leadership – asked for a king, God wearily agreed but warned them that it would end in tears. 'A king,' God said, 'will send your sons to fight wars, tax you heavily, and spend your hard-earned wealth on their own houses until you cry out for relief.' Despite the warning, the people got their kings. Some were just; most were just awful. In the end, God was proved right.

Years later, when disappointment had crushed dreams of glory and empire, a different kind of leader appeared on the scene. He had peculiar politics, but seemed to practice what he preached. For some he was a messiah, for others he was a dangerous liability. He too would walk the fickle tightrope of man's expectation and go from saviour to failure in a matter of days. Yet the scene of his defeat would, his followers believed, turn out to be the scene of his greatest triumph and leave future leaders with an interesting challenge. If you want people to follow you all the way, you have to go there first.

19.1.2010

—

Millions, billions, trillions

I'd like to start by asking you a question. How much time do you think a million seconds is? The answer is eleven-and-a-half days. So, if a million seconds is eleven-and-a-half days, how much time is a billion seconds? The answer is 32 years. When asked this question I was wildly out with my answer, suggesting a billion wasn't much more than a million, and that a trillion wasn't much more than that (a trillion seconds, by the way, is 31,688 years).

In recent years, I've got into the habit of letting these numbers blur into one big 'they're all basically the same' number: so much so that when the government say they're about to make cuts of £6 billion, I can't be sure whether this is an exceptional or perfectly usual amount of money. Billions, trillions, shmillions? I'll let the experts work it out, it's all Greek to me. Which is lazy and probably irresponsible, because it's not just the Greeks who are in debt. Nor is it the experts who will have to pay for ours: it's me, it's you, our children and probably their children, too.

Debt has a habit of causing a vagueness and denial in the debtor. This goes for individuals as much as countries. I've spotted this tendency in my own life. When I know I'm in credit I'm happy to check the amount in my current account at the cashpoint, but as soon as it slips into the red I stop looking and start to guess. It's partly to do with guilt, but it's also connected to a kind of fear that the number will be much bigger than I think – or worse.

Debt looms large in scripture. God commands both individuals and nations to avoid it, not to let others be indebted to them, and to do all they can to get out of it. He seems to care about the numbers, right down to the timeframe and the percentages involved. Yet just when you think God's a parsimonious accountant, he turns out to be an extravagant father.

A 'have-no-debts-at-all' policy becomes an instruction to cancel all outstanding debts every seven years and start again. Thrift becomes largesse.

We see this most potently in the ultimate 'debt-recovery story' of the prodigal son, where one brother blows his inheritance and is welcomed back by his father while the other – who probably knew to the very shekel how much debt his brother had – watches enviously as his dad lets him off. Whatever the rights and wrongs here, both were utterly dependent on the generosity of a father they couldn't repay.

The paradox is that this God, to whom a thousand years is but a day, sees all men as equally indebted. Debt is the bottom line from which we all start, but rather than this being a trap from which we can't escape, it's seen as the place at which recovery starts. It's not that this God doesn't care about the numbers, it's just that when the billions move into the trillions and our indebtedness becomes too big to comprehend, He's already calculated the cost.

19.5.2010

—

Africa's first World Cup

You know that it's coming. The signs are everywhere. Even the sceptics recognize them and unbelievers know what they mean. When the Panini stickers are in the paper shop. A cross of St George has appeared in the back of your neighbour's van, and a key England player has injured his foot.

You know it's coming when the bishop of Croydon is offering a prayer for fans to enjoy the celebration as well as a prayer that non-fans will be granted the gift of sympathy. Or when you've just noticed that if England finish second in their group, their quarter-final will clash with that wedding you're meant to be going to on July 2nd.

You know it's coming when you realize that this is your twelfth World Cup, that you'll be 50 by the time the next one comes around and that you can still recall with mega-pixel precision where you were when Gary Lineker equalized against Germany... and that you actually got on your knees during the penalty shoot-out, even though part of you suspected God didn't really favour the prayers of the English above the prayers of the Germans.

You know that it's coming when it feels like we've been here before even though this is in fact the first World Cup on African soil. A World Cup that some said no African country had a prayer of winning, let alone staging.

You know that it's coming when there are articles about the amazing array of African footballing talent on show and this being Africa's chance to show the world what it can do; countered by pieces about how the money should be spent on better things and the fact that so much of the continent still depends upon our aid.

You know that it's coming when you can feel the tension between the celebration and the cost; the transcendent and the transient; the hope that this sporting event really does do something to change things and the suspicion that it might all be forgotten in a matter of weeks.

You know that it's coming when you sense that it isn't just about football, it's about nations playing together and partying together – even praying together – and that for every one cynic there are ten hopefuls; and that somewhere in Rwanda a kid with an Arsenal shirt is making a ball from a condom and imagining himself scoring the winning goal in the final.

You know that it's coming when, despite the wages of the players, the size of the stadiums or the amount of money that's made from television rights, that it's bigger than all this and that when a president says 'Football is about hope of a better world, hope for youngsters, and that Africa might turn a corner' that, even though it's just words, it might actually be true. For all the humbug, there is hope that, for all the fantasy, there's a reality and that for all the doubt, this is Africa's first World Cup and they do have a prayer.

22.6.2010

—

Not enough Brownie points

This week, some local authorities have been considering the merits of a Japanese system of giving reward points in order to motivate volunteering. Called 'Caring Relationship Tickets' it allows volunteers to bank the hours they spend helping an elderly or disabled person in a personal 'Time Account' and then claim back the credits for their own care later in life.

Whatever its merits, it could spell the end for that other system of accruing points through doing good deeds: Brownie Points. This hypothetical moral currency was probably named after the brown stamps given out in post-war America; although I prefer the theory that they're named after the badges obtained by Brownies, who were themselves named after a mythological elf who does helpful things around the house for nothing.

The trouble is, the elves around our house seem to want payment in a more visible currency. Only this week I paid my son to wash the car and my daughter to do the hoovering, two tasks I'm pretty sure I did for nothing back in the day. Like the government I'm struggling to find a middle way that enables me to be both paternalist and libertarian. Should I nudge the kids into acts of kindness with financial incentives or leave them to do it of their own volition and risk getting nothing done?

Deep down, I'm not sure we can legislate for kindness. Paying people to volunteer sounds like an oxymoron. It would certainly mean re-writing some stories about altruistic deeds: The Good Samaritan wouldn't be the same had his first thought on seeing a battered man in the road been: 'Great, this is a chance for me to top up my Caring Points Card.' We'd also have to adjust the bumper sticker that says, 'Volunteers do it for free,' to include the corollary 'Just as long as there are incentives.'

It's interesting that groups are warning that rewarding voluntary work undermines the idea of giving your time freely. The dynamic of giving without expectation of a return is changed when financial reward is introduced. Like a spiritual Heisenberg Uncertainty Principle, the moment you try and monetize kindness you change its very nature. A few years ago, I met a volunteer in an AIDS programme who had offered his services free for ten years before there was enough money for him to be paid. Although grateful for the salary, he said he'd always felt he had his true reward.

What is the reward if not money? Some might say (as they say of Brownie points) that it's all about looking to others and feeling good about yourself; but as Jesus pointed out, the hypocrites liked to do their good deeds for everyone to see, they already had their reward – namely the approval of men. People don't volunteer because they want recognition; if anything, the incentive lies in its hidden opposite. It's said that the great secret of giving freely is that it is its own reward; the trick (as I keep trying to tell my children) is that you won't know this until you try it.

4.11.2010

—

Remembering Remembrance

Today is Remembrance Day (sometimes known as Poppy Day) and observed in commonwealth countries to remember the sacrifices of members of the armed forces and civilians in times of war. It recalls the eleventh hour of the eleventh day of the eleventh month that marked the official end of World War I.

I say this like a man who knows, but the truth is I had to look it up to remind myself exactly when and what it is I am officially meant to be remembering. Part of my uncertainty over the date stems from the appearance of poppies in lapels and radiator grills as early as mid-October. Like Christmas, the build-up to Remembrance Day seems to start earlier each year and it's another occasion that triggers mild dissent and resistance – as expressed through the non-wearing of poppies – in protest at what some see as an unthinking social conformity, or yet another sacred day that's been drained of its original meaning.

Whether or not we choose to wear poppies, it seems right to try to remember exactly what we are remembering. Remembrance Day is one of those orthodoxies that's easily hijacked by those with other agendas – to help sell newspapers or to stir up national pride. It also lends itself to a confusing mix of emotions and ironies: we want to be proud of 'our boys' (and girls) in the armed forces, but we want to avoid the jingoism that spurs men on to battle. We get caught between honouring the sacrifices made by people fighting in wars that were often futile and fuelled by vanity or hubris, or having to balance feeling grateful for the freedom that was hard-won by others with the freedom to ask whether that is what was achieved.

It seems to me that it's key to the process of remembrance that we wrestle with. Aeschylus wrote that truth was always the first casualty of war, which gives us all the more reason to be rigorous in our remembrance and ask the difficult questions: Why did they die? Did they die in vain? Where was God in all of this? What would those we are trying to remember want us to remember?

In search of answers, we often turn to the witness of those soldier-poets of the First World War – Owen, Graves, Sassoon – and what is so striking about their words is how much of a corrective they are to the sentiment and distortion of fact that war so easily engenders. They remind us with the blunt-brutal authority of men who were there not to fall into the traps of glorifying war while at the same time asking us to remember them – even when they weren't brave, even when they lost their faith, even when they did die in vain. Because it's not the battles won that matters – it is the lives lost – and it's the gift of the living to be able to remember them.

10.11.2010

—

The King James Bible

In the midst of the commemorations surrounding the 400th anniversary of the King James Bible, an orthodoxy seems to be forming; one that unites Southern Baptists, agnostic poets and atheist commentators alike: that this is the finest and most influential Bible translation in English.

For proof, we only have to look to television, the football terraces or the pub and hear that a character is 'the salt of the earth,' or that a certain manager is going 'to reap the whirlwind'; or that 'there's no peace for the wicked,' phrases coined by a remarkable committee of translators 400 hundred years ago that have entered our everyday parlance.

In this sense, the translators fulfilled part of their mission when they stated they wanted 'To make God's holy truth yet more and more known unto the people.' Yet 400 years on, while people are praising the King James' literary brilliance and cultural reach, less has been said of it imparting anything as dangerous as 'God's holy truth.'

Maybe the challenge is to move from an appreciation of how something is being said to what is being said. Even when the right words are in the right order, the Bible – in any translation – is more than literature. As those King James translators themselves worded it in Hebrews: 'The word of God is quick' (a living thing) or God breathed (to use a later translation). It contained a vital message from God to all mankind, a message so important that it needed to be expressed in a language all could understand, and it didn't require wealth or sophistication to hear that it had something very important to say. This was not just a book to be read, it was something to be ingested, and lived. It even had the power to transform.

We need to be careful that by paying homage to the literary excellence and influence of the King James Bible, we don't become like the Pharisees, getting lost in the wordy woods and missing the tree altogether. Like the little girl who, after being read the story of the feeding of the 5,000, asked if it was true, and her father said 'Probably not, but it's a nice story.' To which she replied, 'But it's a much better story if it's true.'

The outstanding achievement of this translation has been its ability to move and speak to an unlikely congregation of believers and unbelievers across four centuries. It is part of the wonder of this book that where one clearly sees *beautiful* words, another clearly sees that God is the word.

It is right to praise those inspired messengers of 400 years ago, but while celebrating the eloquence and majesty of the translation, let us also keep in mind the translators' stated desire that the fruit of this scripture 'Extendeth itself, not only to the time spent in this transitory world, but directeth and dispotheth men unto that eternal happiness which is above in heaven.'

12.1.2011

—

The meaning of statistics

Earlier this week I was discussing climate change with a good friend. At one point I threw a statistic at him to back up a particular argument. I thought it was a trustworthy statistic. Until my friend asked me where I'd got it? The fact is, I couldn't recall. I'd just read it somewhere. A few days later he sent me some data – complete with sources and graphs – that utterly refuted my argument.

Even as I looked at these potentially opinion-changing stats, I found myself resisting the evidence. Not because I didn't understand or trust the sources, but because they didn't fit my preconceived idea of what was true. I might previously have claimed to be 'just interested in the facts and free of any agenda', but the gravitational pull of deeper, irrational forces was warping my perspective, biasing any objectivity I thought I had.

Perhaps we should always be wary of the person who uses statistics to try and win an argument. To quote Auden, 'Out of the air a voice without a face; Proved by statistics that some cause was just.'

Some big, often contingent decisions get made based on statistics: wars are waged, budgets are set. All the more reason, then, to be sure of their accuracy. The problem is even then statistics can mislead. A female driver aged between 20 and 65 will have had fewer accidents than a male of the same age. Does this mean that women are better drivers than men? More seriously, the UK engaged in more armed conflicts than any other country between 1946 and 2005, with a total of 22 (23 if we include Libya). Do we conclude that we are a nation of warmongers or a country that values peace?

Even when we have all the data to hand, something else beyond reason is required for us to build an understanding from the knowledge we have. Watching *The Wonders of the Universe* television series, I have to engage my brain as Professor Brian Cox explains how space time bends. Yet as soon as he says 'There are over a trillion, trillion galaxies out there in infinite space', I have to do something else – I have to engage my imagination to get some perspective on the data.

Scripture points out that 'knowledge puffs up but love builds up.' It suggests that knowledge is not the full picture. It can make us arrogant, deaf to other people's opinions, where love can lead to a greater awareness, a greater wonder and a better understanding. While arguing facts about climate change with my friend, I have to remember what matters – my friend.

It's fascinating that in God's famous answer to Job that begins, 'Where were you when I laid the earth's foundation,' He includes a stunning amount of data about the earth and seas, planets and stars, even galaxies. At one level it reads like someone comprehensively winning the argument with the ultimate statistical proof. At another, it's a reminder to Job – and to all of us – that all the knowledge in the world is worthless without a right perspective.

24.03.2011

—

The only girl in the world

So I was dancing with my 11-year-old daughter to Rihanna's *Only Girl In The World*, singing the chorus, 'Want you to make me feel like I'm the only girl in the world; Like I'm the only one you'll ever love,' while deliberately muffling the next verse about 'Being in command and making you feel like a man,' and telling myself she probably won't understand anyway. Then the next track, *S&M*, came on and my feeling of innocent abandon slowly gave way to a sense of being exploited.

The video for Rihanna's single *S&M* features whips and chains and has been banned in eleven countries. While it's provoked another set of warnings about the sexualization of children, I wonder if the real problem here is a cultural confusion about sex in general. With many woman around the world taking part in the 'Slut walk' protest – triggered when a Canadian policeman told students to avoid dressing like sluts in order avoid being victimized – it feels like we're struggling for clarity and consensus on what sexual health and freedom looks like.

While I applaud the self-expression of a Rihanna or a Lady Gaga, many of their and other pop stars' videos offer an extreme portrayal of a particular vision of sexuality that permeates not just pop, but ads, movies, magazine and newspapers. For me they're often fantasies that dress themselves in the corsets of liberation when, in fact, their real heart is to separate sex from love and intimacy and dominate commercially, caring little if the audience are 11-year-old girls or middle-aged men.

So where do we look for sexual wholeness and integrity in a world that is hooked on imagery that celebrates loveless sex? There are some who would eliminate sex when they speak of love, supposing they're making it more holy. There are others who, when they think of sex, never think of love. When a prostitute entered the house of a Pharisee where Jesus was eating, there was a huge ripple of disapproval in the room. When I read this text, I can almost smell the lust of the men and their hypocritical judgement on her appearance, and can hear them thinking, 'How did she get in here?' All this before she performs this outrageous, sensuous, intimate act of washing Jesus' feet with oil.

Unlike the other men, Jesus – who always had this knack of seeing what was really going on – saw what she really wanted. She wasn't a slut, she was a human being searching for a fuller realization of her humanity – of which her sexuality was but one part – while at the same time desiring an intimacy that wasn't born of exploitation or commercial transaction. She wanted liberation, not bondage. It seemed that until this moment, no one had ever shown her what love looked like. Yet by receiving her and letting her be, Jesus made her feel like she 'was the only girl in the world,' and that he was perhaps 'the only one who would love her.'

18.5.2011

—

Not enough power

The scandal enveloping Newscorp is playing like a drama that's hard to categorize. It's blockbuster, soap opera, morality play, family saga, political theatre and a police story all rolled into one. It's gripping for all kinds of reasons and not all of them noble – it's shocking, brazen, unsubtle and spiced with hubris, schadenfreude, revenge and justice, and it seems all the more dramatic because no-one saw it coming, even though some of the writing had been on the wall for months, even years.

If it's about one thing it's about power: Who has it? How much should they have? What are they doing with it? The apostle John suggested that the three basic areas of temptation are sex, money and power – and while much of human existence involves a struggle with one or all three of these things, power is by far the most dangerous, mainly because it's so hard to measure: we know when we're having sex and we can count our money, but no one can say for sure how much power they have – few believe they have enough.

In some ways, most of us want the world to bend to our will. I imagine that, most days, a media mogul asks the same question you or I might ask: 'Do I have the power I need to achieve my aims?' Its temptations operate at every scale of life – in the home, at work, in school – luring us into that subtlest of traps where we set ourselves us up over someone else to get what we want. It's why we must handle whatever power we've been given with the greatest care and respect.

Indeed, if we see power as a gift, rather than something we earn, we might well be protecting ourselves from its most corrosive qualities. Power – political, cultural, domestic – can and should be creative, shared and given away. If it isn't, we end up chasing it for its own sake, we start believing our own hype and become a law unto ourselves. Like the people of Babel who said, 'Let us build a city, a tower; and then let us make a name for ourselves', in trying to secure power we end up forgetting where true power comes from in the first place.

Which brings us to a key question: Where does true power come from and what does it look like? Is it something we create, or is it a gift from a power greater than ourselves? In a seemingly unsensational moment in the gospels, Jesus reminded his disciples that, through relationship with him, they had access to the ultimate power in the universe. Yet before they could get carried away with thoughts of conquering and dominating the world, He told them what to do with it. Give it away, he said. Share it; not because it's too dangerous to handle, but because that's the way true power works.

13.7.2011

—

Apprentices

When Tom Pellereau won the final of *The Apprentice* earlier this week, it was described as a victory for the nice guy. A competition that usually rewards the robotically determined, pushy type had seen a more personable, unassuming contestant win through. Interestingly, when interviewed afterwards on the sister show *You're Fired*, he didn't seem that different to the person we'd seen on the main show. He'd somehow managed to remain true to who he was throughout the whole thing.

It was also striking how much more likeable *all* the contestants were once released from the pressure cooker of the competition; the show demands ruthlessness from its contestants and it's edited to exaggerate this, but it did seem that too many of them had tried to live up to someone else's idea of what they should be rather than trusting in being the person they were. Perhaps this is why Lord Sugar hired who he did. He saw through the tactic of trying to win by being something you're not.

Such an approach may be harmless in the world of entertainment, but in the real world of work– where the pressures to succeed and the temptations to win approval are greater – it can be hugely destructive. People are in such a hurry to get on they forget who they are; they magnify themselves by imitating what they think will make them popular. They may even gain a modicum of success by adopting this strategy – might even be applauded for their go-gettingness – but in the process they lose something far more valuable, namely their integrity; that sense of self, or wholeness that's essential for well-being; something not based an outward appearance, but on an internal consistency. What scripture describes as 'Truth in the inner most parts.'

Keeping our integrity under pressure is harder work than we might think. Remaining true to yourself especially when you're desperate for work, when competition is so great, or when people are asking you tough questions that expose your weaknesses, sometimes requires real calm as well as a fair amount of courage and humility. Yet it's under pressure that we find out just how 'whole' we are, or how much integrity we really have.

The would-be apprentices following Jesus were often looking for the quick route to glory and tempted to hurry through to victory without wanting to do the hard-yards. Under pressure, they'd even deny and dissemble to get their way. Yet their Master was forever setting them straight; not by firing the weak, self-regarding or selfish candidates (he'd have had few followers taking that approach), but by letting them make their inevitable mistakes and then taking the time to show them and teach them who they really were. In his company, there was absolutely nothing to be gained by being inauthentic or taking short cuts, but everything to be gained by facing up to the truth of who we are. Victory for the Nice Guy.

21.7.2011

—

Tax rating

In a world where a reported 10 per cent of the population earns over half of the income, the other 90 per cent must be hoping that the 10 per cent are the kind of people inclined to share it out. Yet what happens if the richest people in the world don't want to?

I've always thought this where tax came in. A kind of check to our disinclination to share. You can't legislate for generosity, but you can protect people against a lack of it. There's scant evidence to show that people become more munificent the wealthier they get. My own income has risen for the last ten years; but the proportion I give has stayed the same. If anything I'm now more likely to look for tax efficient ways of keeping it; more tempted to store it away for rainy days than use it to cover someone else's head.

With the major capitalist economies grappling with massive deficits, tax has suddenly become the big issue. While we debate the merits of a 50 per cent income tax rate, President Obama is trying to implement a 'Buffet Rule' that would see anyone earning over a $1 million a year pay the same rate as those earning much less. It's named after billionaire Warren Buffet, who was so embarrassed at paying less tax than the people who worked in his office that he said: 'It was time his government got serious about shared-sacrifice.'

That's an interesting euphemism: tax as shared sacrifice. Tax is usually a punitive term; indeed, what is seen as a necessary corrective to some is an evil imposition to others. Buffet's comment implies we need to see tax in a new way. Sitting at a harvest thanksgiving service this weekend it occurred to me that an industrialized, urban society still has something to learn from the ploughing of fields, the scattering of seeds and the sharing of crops. In such cultures a harvest was everyone's to receive and enjoy; it was a terrible iniquity if it wasn't shared out and it perished if it wasn't.

Jesus offered no comment on his preferred tax rates, but whether people earned mites or millions he seemed to have a definite view on what we should do with our wealth. As the parable of the rich man, who built a bigger barn to store up his extra goods, brutally illustrates: holding on to it is not a healthy option: on the very night that the rich man was congratulating himself on having enough wealth for years to come, he died.

If we're ever going to change these dismal statistics of inequality, it seems some level of self-sacrifice has to play a part. The biggest obstacle to this is thinking we will lose everything if we take such an approach. Yet the parable suggests this is a mistake. It's not that God needs our money or our stuff; it's about transforming us into the kind of people who are inclined to share all they can. In the end it's not how much we have, it's what we do with it.

20.9.2011

Too small to fail

With the Italian economy on the brink, the phrase 'too big too fail' is getting a lot of air-time. It's been floating around public discourse ever since the last financial crisis three years ago when a bank, that was supposedly too big to fail, failed. Yet it's more than just a colloquial term. It's a theory in which certain financial institutions are deemed to be so large and interconnected that they must receive beneficial policies to keep them alive. Their bigness, if you like, must be protected at all costs because their demise would apparently be a disaster for us all.

Given the long history of really big things failing, it's odd that this kind of thinking still has such credence. Lehman Brothers, Enron, General Motors, Real Madrid, The Titanic, The Roman Empire, The Tower of Babel. That dinosaur whose head got too big for its body. The list of things or people deemed way too strong, too successful, too rich, too important to fail but did is, well, enormous.

It suggests that our reverence for the big isn't some kind of sophisticated economic principle, but something quite primitive and irrational. Mankind may have stopped worshipping the monolith, but he still adores the monolithic. Big is best. Might is right. In large we trust. The great danger of this is delusion. Like the fading actress in *Sunset Boulevard* who, when told 'You used to be big,' replies, 'I am big. It's the pictures that got small.' Pride inverts our perspective. We are no longer able to see the pathway to redemption, because it seems too small and insignificant to us.

Could it be that size isn't all its bigged-up to be? Even Allan Greenspan, former chairman of the Federal Reserve, implied that there were limits to scale when he said, 'If they're too big to fail, they're too big.' What if we inverted the phrase and said of countries, or companies, or even people that they were 'too small to fail.' Instead of protecting the powerful from their own failures we let them fail in order for small things to make their way in the world, not out of some romantic egalitarianism, but because small really is beautiful – and is where the foundations of our welfare and wellbeing lie.

When people built the tower of Babel and said, 'Let us build a city with a tower that reaches to the heavens,' they were sure their project was too big to fail. Seeing their hubris, God intervened, confused their languages, and the people were scattered all over the world as a result. His interjection is sometimes perceived negatively, but by letting Babel fail, God was actually scattering the seeds of a future hope. While man's big plans lay in monolithic ruin, God's plan was only just beginning. Man wanted to get to God by bigging himself up, but God's plan involved a total inversion of this. To save mankind He had to make himself too small to fail.

9.11.2011

—

Resolutions

There was once a man who, on the last day of every year, made a list of resolutions for the year to come. Now this man was no fool. He knew what structured reality was. He knew that the God Particle probably had nothing to do with God, and that a Bond yield wasn't something Daniel Craig earned every year.

He believed Chesterton's dictum that 'unless a man starts afresh about things, he will do nothing effective.' Yet he also knew how difficult it was to keep even one resolution. He'd blown his first resolution to drink less beer in the first week of January; and his plan to read the Bible in a year by the second. His weight loss regime lasted a fat month.

This year was going to be different. Being a year of cut-backs, he decided to restrict himself to one, gettable resolution; one that would make him a better person (for deep down this is what he wanted). Yet as he tried to visualize his perfected self – a vision in which he was always slim, fit, knowledgeable, healthy, well-informed and generally maximizing his key deliverables – the image was vague and hard to see.

Instead, the ghosts of new year's resolutions past whispered their humbug wit. There was Mark Twain telling him he'd be paving hell with his resolutions before the week was out. Burns with his line about Mice and Men and best laid schemes. Some even said that the best way to make God laugh was to tell him your plans.

By now the man was in a fearful funk. He didn't know what to write. Meanwhile, the last day of the year ticked out its final seconds in its indifferent, callous way. 'Why do we even celebrate a passage of time when it wouldn't give us the time of day?' the man thought as he stared at the blank page of his potential year, his resolution unresolved.

Desperate for guidance, he asked the Great God Google for help, but after typing the word 'resolution' into the search engine, he discovered that people were making the same kind of vows as him – and that most were failing to keep them. All over the world, people were fighting a war with their vices and they were losing.

On the verge of giving up he looked up the definition of resolution and discovered that it came from the Latin and meant to loosen or release. Absently he scribbled the word release on the still-blank page, and as he stared at it he thought how much he'd like to be released from this annual ritual, from the treadmill of trying and failing, from the burning thirst for success, ambition and pleasure. Released, too, from the predictions of economic gloom and ecological disaster, from the threat of pain, sickness and death. Yet what resolution could possibly set him free from this?

The year was almost over. The Bible he'd given up reading after two weeks sat on his desk, reminding him of his failure. Annoyed he opened it and, feeling like a cheat reader wanting to know the end, he turned to the reading for December 31st, and there, in the last paragraph of the last page of the last book, was the line, 'God will dwell with men. He will wipe away every tear from their eyes, there shall be no more death, no more sorrow, no crying, no more pain because the former things have passed away.' With that, he closed the book and left the room.

3.1.2012

—

How much do you earn?

If you're ever at a dinner party and the conversation is getting dull, and people start talking about schools or showing funny clips from the Internet because you've run out of things to say, just ask the guests how much they earn. I guarantee this will either lead to the complete death of the evening or, perhaps, to a proper grown-up conversation about money and values, maybe even life itself.

My wife did this recently and after everyone had finished choking on their lemon chicken, it opened up a dicey but meaningful discussion. The question may have been a bit rude and one or two (noticeably the wealthier) reserved the right not to disclose their earnings, but behind the whole thing there was a desire to break a taboo – the sacred cow of personal finances – and ask some important questions: How *do* we earn our money? What do we do with it? How much is enough?

Questions that have come into sharp focus this week with the announcement that the chief executive of RBS Bank, Stephen Hester, is being paid a £1 million bonus on top of his £1 million salary. Judging from the outcry, most people seem to think that this is more than enough, for him or anyone.

Keeping bankers accountable is a good thing, but I think there's a complicated mix of a desire for fairness and old-fashioned envy at work here. In the middle of this opprobrium, it would be a shame to miss asking ourselves the same question: How much is enough?

So how much is enough? One proverb suggests that not too much and not too little is not a bad place to start: 'Give me neither poverty nor riches, but give me only my daily bread. For riches come with their own troubles.' Another suggests that large salaries are not to be envied because, 'the abundance of a rich man permits him no sleep.' I don't know how well Mr Hester is sleeping, but if we are up all night thinking about *his* millions, while bemoaning the lack of our own, are we any better off?

In the end, it's not what we earn that defines us. It's how we earn it and, more importantly, what we do with it. A poor man won't sleep any better for envying the rich man, while a rich man's abundance might not keep him awake at night if he does something interesting with it.

I *want* to live in a society that asks how much is enough; and I *want* to sit at the table and never be afraid to ask what someone earns, how they earn it and what they do with it. If we can be more accountable with the person whom we sit next to at dinner, perhaps we'll be better equipped to make decisions for society at large. So, let's keep having the conversation.

28.1.2012

—

In Bruges

Last week I was in Bruges. We were standing in front of yet another unbelievably stunning painting by the Flemish artist Hans Memling, in a twelfth-century hospital built specifically for the poor, when my daughter said, 'Oh no, another picture of Jesus. Did they ever paint anything else?'

I had to laugh. Although I knew that most artists of the fifteenth century were obliged to paint religious scenes and that these were some of the best ever painted, I shared her complaint. For the last hour we'd gone from one brilliant depiction of the infant Jesus to another, without a profane image in sight. The whole town was saturated in a heavy religious culture. The accumulative effect was becoming monotonous, even oppressive.

Which got me thinking: if someone who *believes* in what's being depicted in these paintings is struggling to connect with their spiritual content, perhaps all this rich culture is obscuring rather than enhancing the story that inspired it. Is it possible to find the spark of faith in it, or has it been snuffed out by the weight of tradition and history? Could I even spot the difference?

As we continued walking through the city, I played a game, trying to separate what I thought was inspired by a true faith in God and what was not. It quickly became difficult: for every almshouse there was a wealthy patron who'd paid for it; the money made in the market might have raised the tower in the square, but it also bankrolled the foundling homes and the schools. Neither were the great paintings done *pro bono*. After a while I gave up, it was impossible to tell. This city, like many great European cities, was a complex meld of venal ambition, artistic brilliance, social climbing and sincere kindness and charity. Faith was in the mix, some of it pure some of it bogus. Yet it wasn't easy to separate the human from the divine. A bit like life.

In his recent biography, the former Bishop of Edinburgh, Richard Holloway, identifies this tension when he writes, 'My mistake was to think religion was more than human.' He goes on: 'I was less sure whether God was also just a human invention, but I was sure religion was.' As with the art and architecture of Christendom, much of it obviously a human construct, it's sometimes hard to know where *God* is in it all.

Yet Paul once described Jesus as 'The invisible image of God for whom all things – visible and invisible – were created.' This cosmic claim reminds us that when God got involved with humanity, he also got involved with culture. I confess, I found it hard to match the image of Jesus, so skillfully depicted by Memling, with the image I carry in my head. Perhaps that's how it's meant to be – a messy mix of imperfect people trying to imagine and interpret a perfect God who can never be perfectly pictured.

20.2.2012

—

Truth to power

The reporter Marie Colvin, who was killed in Homs last week, once said that her mission was to 'speak truth to power.' After a brilliant and colourful career reporting on conflicts in Bosnia, Chechnya and, fatally, in Syria, it was an ideal for which she paid the highest price.

Speaking truth to power sounds like something from a Greek tragedy or Shakespearian history play, but its first recorded use was as the title of a Quaker pamphlet written in 1955, one of a series of documents that challenged US Cold War policy by trying to articulate to the powers that be a gentle reprimand and a different approach.

However, speaking truth to power isn't limited to the heroes of reportage or political dissent; it's something we all get the opportunity to do, often in the most mundane of everyday interactions and in the most subtle of circumstances. The boss who misrepresents the situation in a meeting, the father who shuts down his child's justified protest, or the friend who's a little lax with the facts.

Yet it's hard to do. I've watched a bullying boss verbally abuse a colleague and done nothing. I've listened to the vicar talk drivel and remained silent over coffee afterwards. When presented with the opportunity to speak out, I've backed away – because I was afraid to, or I didn't want to upset anyone, or I told myself it wasn't worth the grief.

The need for people to speak truth becomes even more urgent when we are the ones with power. Hopefully we all have friends or colleagues who will tell us when we're talking nonsense or being controlling. We certainly need them, because the number of people willing to challenge you with the truth surely goes down in inverse proportion to your power. It's so much more tempting, and easier, to say something flattering.

When King Lear's favourite daughter, Cordelia, doesn't tell him what he wants to hear, she sets in motion the tragic spiral of events that, although appalling, ultimately leads to him seeing the truth. For Lear, truth and power needed to be brutally separated before he can recognize the difference. I could be that we all have to de-throne ourselves to see it.

Jesus was brought before Pilate for speaking truth to power, and it was Pilate – the man seemingly with the power – who asked him what truth was. Jesus answered him by saying nothing, letting truth speak for itself. When he'd taken on the religious authorities, Jesus had quoted Jeremiah, accusing them of making God's house 'a den of thieves;' by doing this he was identifying himself with a man who had to shout *his* truth to power from a cesspit in the city's sewers. It was a hint that if you're going to do it, don't expect everyone to love or reward you for it. Sometimes you have to give up your power in order for other people to hear the truth.

28.2.2012

—

Time to play

On Bank Holiday Monday I went for an early morning walk. There was one other person in the park, a man walking his dog. 'Happy Easter' I said as I passed him. 'What's to be happy about?' he fired back with some feeling. If I'd had my wits about me I might have said, 'Well, you know: Jesus conquering death, rising again: that sort of thing,' but that wasn't it. He was just upset about the money that the 'flipping bank holiday' was costing him.

Before I could quote the proverb, 'Better one handful with tranquillity than two hands with toil and chasing after the wind,' he was gone; and so was I, back to my office to get on with my day's work. For, like him, I'd had enough of holidays. I'd spend the last week in Cornwall sort of working, sort of resting, and it hadn't been productive. I needed to make up for lost time.

The low value that we both put on our rest time was amplified at the macro level this week when an economic think-tank – citing the connection between Korea's improved GDP and increased working hours – suggested we would be better off if we worked longer and had fewer holidays. Perhaps if the purpose of our existence lay in boosting Gross Domestic Product this would be a sound policy. We could probably cut weekends while we're at it. The trouble is that GDP, as Bobby Kennedy pointed out, measures everything except that which makes life worthwhile.

If scripture is to be believed, God values rest far more than we do. Presumably aware of our tendency to overdo things, He made it a commandment, suggesting we take at least one day off a week – even during the busiest times – and promising to make it worth our while. This was not so much a protestant work ethic, more a divine rest ethic. An economy where GDP might have stood for God Demands Playtime or Get Dancing, People.

This bank holiday – indeed every holiday – is haunted by the ghost of its original purpose: a holy day in which people enjoy the source of that holiness. Rest is not simply respite from work, or a period that enables us to go back to work even harder, it is an end in itself. It's not an escape from reality, but an actual picture of it in which play, laughter, creativity and being together is the work. Rest might even hint at what the purpose of our existence is.

Somewhere in my head there's still this formula that says work equals money, rest equals a missed opportunity. Yet as my unproductive working holiday proved, not resting is often a false economy. After all, there's little point in lying down in green pastures or beside still waters if I'm too busy to let God restore my soul.

12.4.2012

—

An untrue story

I was recently at a private function that was reported in a national newspaper by a journalist who clearly wasn't at the event. The presence of a few celebrities had made some sort of speculative coverage inevitable, but the paper's description of what happened bore little relation to the reality. Mixed in with some general facts, the article mentioned the names of people who weren't there and things that didn't happen, and it did so with the authority and certainty of a trustworthy witness. It was convincing enough for a couple of friends to ring and ask me if those things were really true.

Some will say it doesn't really matter if a newspaper takes half a page to tell its readers about an event without actually telling the whole truth. Why let a few facts get in the way of a good story? Just as long as nothing unpleasant is said, nothing is written than might lead to a lawsuit. If people are entertained enough, who cares? They shouldn't believe everything they read in newspapers anyway.

Except that people – me included – often do: trivial things, profound things. What people read helps form judgement and shape opinion, which is why it's so vital that papers take truth seriously. This is a week in which the Leveson Inquiry reaches a key phase, and if it has shown us anything it is the importance – both to society and the individual – of a reliable and trustworthy witness. It might seem wise not to believe everything you read, but it's good not to have to doubt the veracity of everything that's printed. There are some stories that are too important not to be trusted.

For instance, if you read a story about a private function where, towards the end of the evening, a man turned six vats of water in to wine, you'd probably want to get a few facts straight: Where was did this happen? What day was it? What did the wine taste like? How much water did he change? Perhaps most importantly, Who was this guy? Such an event is, of course, reported in some detail in John's Gospel. It was a wedding that took place on a Tuesday in Cana, where a man turned 180 gallons of water into a wine so good the host asked why the best stuff had been kept until last. As for the man's name…

Of course, there's every chance that someone made all of this up for the sake of a good story. Yet for some reason it's a story a lot of people still, 2,000 years on, believe and take seriously. If you were looking for symbolic proof of this, you need look no further than the Leveson Inquiry itself. For it's a story that appears in the book that most witnesses – media moguls, ministers and movie stars – place their hand on when they swear to tell the truth, the whole truth and nothing but the truth.

25.4.2012

—

A tale of two thieves

I was burgled this week. I was in the house when it happened, working in my office, oblivious to the fact that two men had broken in. Only when I got up to stretch my legs did I notice one of them coming down the stairs. He looked as surprised as me and shouted to his friend. Moments later, the other man appeared with a bag full of my belongings.

Some part of me said, 'Don't try to stop them,' so I backed into the garden to let them escape. They left and I followed them into the street to try and get a decent look at them. I then called the police and went back to the house to see what they'd done. Even with my interruption, they'd taken a fair bit of stuff and managed to turn most of the rooms upside-down.

A burglary is often described as being a violation, and that's a good word for it because it's not just about what is physically taken, it's about what is emotionally done to the person being robbed. I had suffered no physical assault, but when I sat down to describe what I could to the police over a strong cup of tea, I felt as though I'd been beaten up.

The hurt wasn't really to do with the things that had been stolen (most of that is replaceable and insured), it wasn't the ransacking of personal property, or the time-consuming pain of having to fill out claim forms. It was more the unsettling questions that the burglary had stirred up: What if they'd been armed? What if they come back? Why did this happen?

There was a fear that lingered long after the thieves have fled. Even when writing this (on the laptop that wasn't stolen), I was more conscious of noises coming from the street, suspicious of a person walking a little too slowly up my road. I even bolted the door. I can get all the super-duper alarm systems I like, but will they take away my fear? I'm angry at those thieves for taking my things, but I'll be more annoyed if they rob me of my peace.

Later, as I walked around the house performing a grudging exorcism, I found myself half-praying, half-complaining, wondering what, if anything, God was going to do about it. Of course, I wanted them arrested and my stuff returned, but all I could imagine Him saying was, 'Do not be anxious, don't store up treasures on earth where thieves break in' and then perhaps asking me to pray for the two thieves – something I really wasn't ready to do.

Could it be that the only way to dispel the fear is to imagine how God thinks about them. What is the best outcome – punishment or mercy?

There are those who believe in a God who goes after people. Seizes hold of them, turns them around and changes them. He even invites them into his home. Yet for that door to be open you'd need someone who was prepared to die for a thief. What kind of God would do that?

3.5.2012

—

Tough love

When you hear the word 'welfare' what do you picture? A society that values the well-being of its individuals, where the needs of the poor and vulnerable are met? Or a society where people are reduced to a state of dependency and, like some character from *Shameless*, take advantage of other people's generosity and get away with it?

The term 'welfare' no longer means what it used to. What was once a celebrated ideal for some has become a dirty word for others, and this is a real problem when it comes to wrestling with what is one of the more pressing questions of our day: How do we provide a fair level of support for the vulnerable in an age of austerity?

In the current debate about how much to spend on welfare it seems to me that we need to avoid falling into two different but equally nasty traps: the trap of encouraging a culture of entitlement and dependency on the one hand, against creating a culture of indifference and exploitation on the other.

There is plenty of discussion about levels of spending (and this is where party lines fall hardest), but perhaps we need to focus our energies on trying to define exactly who the vulnerable are. If we can find a measure of consensus and wisdom on this, we might get beyond the partisan to the root issue of who really needs help.

Yet it's complex. Dealing with people who abuse the system is an obvious place to start; but let's not assume that everyone is a deliberate slacker. We might agree that the elderly or disabled are worthy of help, but what about the man who has a job that doesn't pay his rent, or the homeless sojourner that's escaped atrocities in another country? Are we to deny them our support?

Scripture is tough on both the extremes of indulgence and indifference, telling the idler to consider the ant as an example of hard work; while pointing out that Sodom and Gomorrah was destroyed, less for its debauchery, but more for being overfed and under-concerned. However, it also has a very broad, liberal definition of who the vulnerable are: as well as the widows and orphans, it includes aliens, exploited workers and divorcees in its remit. The implication is always that our welfare is intimately bound with their welfare, that if we fail in our duty to look out for these people, there will be consequences for society.

For practical purposes, someone has to decide where the line falls between those who need help and those who don't. Let's really debate the line and, in the process, keep asking, Is our generosity perpetuating rather than solving the problem? Or is our tough love really a hardening of the heart; our frugality a cover for meanness? The apostle Paul exhorts, 'The strong to bear with the failings of the vulnerable,' so let us be sure we know exactly who the vulnerable are.

28.6.2012

—

Homeless opera

A former cabinet minister once infamously described the homeless as 'The people you step over when you're coming out of the opera'. As reprehensible a joke as it is, his words are about to be thrown back at him – or rather sung back – by the kind of people he once stepped over.

This week, Streetwise Opera, a company made up of homeless and ex-homeless players, is set to perform at the Royal Opera House as part of the London 2012 festival build up to the Olympic Games. According to its founder, it's the first time the homeless have been part of an Olympic Games and not been 'Overlooked, made unwelcome, or moved on.'

The salutary thing about this story is that the people you and I, or even ministers, might be 'stepping over' almost certainly aren't who we think they are. The Streetwise Opera itself includes three ex-servicemen, an architect, two music teachers who, for different reasons, found themselves without a home and on the street.

The idea that the homeless are different to the likes of us is really a failure of imagination. It's also a very dangerous way of thinking. As the latest national statistics released in June show, the number of homeless in England has risen by almost a fifth compared with the same period last year. Homelessness isn't something that happens to other people.

A few years ago, I stepped over someone lying in a stairwell in Piccadilly. I was so full of my own concerns I didn't see a person, just an obstacle to get around. After walking about 50 yards I thought, what am I doing? I went back and asked him what he needed. It wasn't a great question. It was -3 degrees. 'A decent sleeping bag would be a start,' he said. I went to Lilywhites and got him a tog factor 12 sleeping bag. When I returned we talked, and he told me he'd once been a soldier. What he really needed was to work again.

There's a story in Matthew's Gospel that's always kept me guessing. It's both comfort to those in need and a warning to those who think they've got it sorted. It's the one where Jesus separates the sheep from the goats, and it suggests that eternal life isn't dependent on how religious we are, but whether we've actually fed the one who is hungry, invited the stranger into our house, or clothed the person in need of clothes. Because, He points out, if we are doing it to them, we are doing it to Him.

The next time we pass someone in a stairwell, it's worth thinking about who we might be stepping over. They may well be homeless, but they might also be an ex-soldier, a former teacher or a future opera singer; perhaps most crucially of all, they could be you, they could be me, or even God Himself.

5.7.2012

—

Save The Children

For the first time in its 100-year history, the charity Save The Children has launched an appeal for children living in the UK as opposed to the developing world. It's done this in response to a report that shows that 1.6 million of our children are now living in poverty, regularly going without a meal, new clothes and heating and living in families earning less than £17,000 a year.

In the same week another group of charities, the governing body of independent schools, has made an appeal to the government asking for it to protect their charitable status and requesting financial support so as to be able to offer assisted places to children from poor backgrounds. Places which can cost parents, in the case of the top private schools, up to £30,000 a year per child.

Both have valid claims, but it seems obvious to me which of the two is a more pressing and deserving case. Yet it's the appeal to help impoverished children that's causing the most heated debate, with some people even threatening to withdrawn support from the charity because they think they're being too 'political'.

Could it be that the gulf between rich and poor has become so great that we've lost some perspective on where the real need lies? While on one side of town private schools may worry about filling their places; on the other, children wonder whether to forgo a lunch in order to buy new shoes.

As a nation, we've got good pedigree in the sphere of charitable giving. Indeed, most current private schools were originally created for the education of the poor. Perhaps the most famous of them, an establishment that has provided 19 Prime Ministers, is Eton College. Founded by Henry VIth as a charitable school to provide free education to 70 boys who could not otherwise afford it. To this day, 20 per cent of its pupils are still offered assisted places.

Some might quote Jesus and say that the poor will always be with us, but he meant it as a statement of truth, not a manifesto. He was also quoting Deuteronomy, which goes on to say, 'I command you to be open handed towards your brothers and the poor and needy; not to be hard hearted or tight fisted but freely lend whatever he needs.' We may not have made poverty history, but we can still aspire to seek its alleviation.

These same principles still inform many of our charitable institutions. On the current website for Eton college, there's declaration of what it is looking for in its pupils. It says this: 'By the time he leaves the school, we want each boy to have that true sense of self-worth which will enable him to stand up for himself and for a purpose greater than himself, and, in doing so, to be of value to society.'

This is a noble aspiration, but it's surely one we should endeavour to extend to all our children whether they can afford it or not.

7.9.2012

—

Admitting mistakes

Certain appalling events in history stay with us in the form of particular images, and in the case of the Hillsborough disaster the image that sticks in my mind is that of fans being pulled to the safety of the upper tier by the people above, and of a man on the pitch weeping over his stricken friend.

It is 23 years since 96 Liverpool fans were crushed to death inside the Sheffield Wednesday stadium at the beginning of the FA Cup semi-final. Only now, though, with the release of previously unseen government papers and the report by the Hillsborough Independent Panel, do we know what really happened that day.

The report demonstrates a shameful litany of human error, some of it unwitting, some of it deliberate. Yet what has been most shocking is the revelation that the police and other emergency services made 'strenuous attempts' to cover up their mistakes and deflect the blame for the disaster onto the innocent fans.

The reaction has been understandably emphatic, ranging from the Prime Minister in parliament apologizing on behalf of the nation for the failure of successive governments to see justice done, to many people vehemently calling for retribution. What is profoundly impressive is the reaction of the actual families involved.

For 23 years they have been seeking justice. Many of them parents who've lost children and had to suffer their reputations being deliberately impugned. Yet, as the chair of the panel, James Jones, the Bishop of Liverpool, said, these families have had to live with an open wound for all this time, and still they have shown a dignified determination to get to the truth.

For them this has not been about retribution, it's been about responsibility. An attitude epitomized by Margaret Aspinall, Chairwoman of the Hillsborough Families Support Group (whose son James died that day) when she said of the report: 'This is what the families and the fans have been fighting for 23 years. Without the truth, you cannot grieve and where there is deceit, you get no justice.'

The human incapacity to admit wrong, our quickness to blame others and cover up, lies at the very heart of this and all human tragedy. It was fear of admitting mistakes that compounded the lie that led to innocents dying and then being blamed for their own deaths. It's a force that propels a thousand injustices. It can only be countered by some mechanism that involves a revealing of wrongdoing, confession and the hope of forgiveness.

The truth sets you free, but liberation does not come without pain. Jesus, before his own death where he was wounded and crushed, told his disciples that even though they would suffer they would not be left alone with their tears. Something with the heart of this gospel is still sung on the terraces of Liverpool FC to this day: 'Walk on, walk on, with hope in your heart. And you'll never walk alone.'

12.9.2012

—

'Do you know what matters in life, Rhidian?'

If you were searching for spiritual insight, the last place you'd think to look would be in the psychiatric wing of your local hospital. It's in just such a place that I've recently learned some unexpected truths about life, God and myself.

A few weeks ago, I was buying a paper at the corner shop when a man came towards me and shook my hand. He told me his full name and said that he liked smoking and cars. He then insisted that I come to his place for a cup of tea.

'His place' was the hospital, just a few yards from my house. I set off the next day, taking gifts of tobacco and a car magazine, feeling pleased about the good turn I was performing. Not only was I making a sacrifice of time, I was going to impart some clarity, some normality – maybe even some healing. My attitude was that of the person about to dispense some kind of blessing.

My new friend was in the garden. A nurse kindly made us tea and we were joined by two other patients. I found myself being asked the most direct and uninhibited questions: Are you religious? What are your credentials for being here today? Are you married? Does your wife mind you growing a beard? I tried to answer them: I have faith but I'm not religious; I'm here because I had been invited; and yes, my wife would probably kiss me a lot more if I didn't have a beard.

Then, after about half an hour, one of the patients said: 'Do you know what matters in life, Rhidian?' 'What's that?' I asked. 'That you love and know that you are loved.' He quoted from the first letter of John: 'God is love and whoever lives in love, lives in God, and God in Him.' 'I agree,' I said. Yet before I left to get back to my normal life, he advised me, 'Remember: be slow to chide and quick to bless.'

I don't want to poeticize mental illness or underplay its prevalence. A recent survey states that one in four of us will experience it in some form. The fact is, my scripture-quoting friend is not allowed to go anywhere without a nurse and has been hospitalized for 20 years; I have no illusions about his vulnerability or dependence. Yet the whole encounter challenged my assumptions about where honesty and insight might be found, blurring the boundaries between what's healthy and what's sick, what's sacred and what's profane.

I shouldn't be surprised; Jesus himself was denounced as a madman. At the time, some said he was 'Demon possessed and raving mad, why listen to him?'

Today, when looking for a spiritual encounter, we are still more likely to head for the professionally holy, to the churches and cathedrals with their comforting rituals, rather than the company of the broken and the unwell. Despite this, I've been back to the hospital, and I intend to keep going. Not because I've got anything to give, but simply because I've discovered a quite unexpected source of blessing.

12.11.2012

Confession over coffee

Every Saturday, after some exercise, I meet a friend for coffee and we get exercised about the evils and injustices of the world. Clearly, we shall never, ever run out of things to get angry about. Even a supposedly uneventful news week gives us bombs in Syria, more child abuse, avoidable deaths from flooding and, as if this isn't enough, press corruption.

My friend gets pretty worked up about these things: 'How can they get away with it? They should fine them, they should put them away, they should execute them.' Sometimes, when he runs out of people to blame or events to get cross about, he might get angry at the non-intervention of a God who lets these terrible things happen in the first place.

Of course, some of this anger is motivated by a genuine compassion and sympathy, and by a desire for justice to be done. However, it's interesting how quickly two men, claiming a hope for a better world, degenerate into lashing out punitively or, frustrated at their powerlessness to do anything about it, give up trying. When our protests don't reach beyond the level of angry reaction our righteous anger soon becomes self-righteous.

What is a creative response to the litany of bad news presented to us on a daily basis? How can we remain open to all these human tragedies without becoming mentally paralysed or depressed? If a misanthropic withdrawal from the world isn't the answer, and blaming people or God gets nothing done, what are we to do?

Perhaps the answer starts with us making a connection between the nature of events and the true nature of our hearts. Is the deception revealed by a Leveson Inquiry, or the violence of a Syria, or the lust and prurience driving so much cultural gossip so far from what's going on inside us? It seems dishonest, maybe even deluded, to think so. The theologian, Henri Nouwen, wrote that 'The cruel reality of the world is the cruel reality of the human heart, our own included.'

Making this connection requires some form of individual confession, and that doesn't come easily – even between the best of friends. We don't often think of our personal confession as having a wider effect, but two people in a café admitting to their own anger, mistakes or lusts can bring a liberation that connects them with the bigger picture. As it says in the letter of James, 'Confess your sins to each other so that you may be healed.'

It's easier, even preferable, to rant about the world's problems, but if we can find a way to confess our own involvement in the mess of humanity, then we should be able to find the remedy for our ills as well as the justice we seek for others.

29.11.2012

—

Pi in the sky

'I have a story that will make you believe in God.' These are the words of the protagonist in *Life of Pi*, the supposedly unfilmable novel that's now been made into a dazzling film by director Ang Lee.

It tells the story of Pi Patel, a shipwrecked boy, floating across the Pacific in a lifeboat with various zoo animals, including a 450-pound Bengal tiger. After a fantastical voyage full of suffering, wonder and existential torment, Pi is washed up in Mexico where he has to explain to the authorities what happened.

At first, they don't believe him and suspect his story is a metaphor for something unpalatable. Yet when Pi gives them a less fantastic version, they dislike it so much they accept the original account as the truth because, they say, 'It's a better story.'

'And so it goes with God,' Pi replies, suggesting that while life is full of suffering it is made more bearable if God is included in the narrative – even if He's a beautiful illusion.

I'm not sure this story would make me believe in a God, but it raises interesting theological questions. Is the better story the beautiful one or the true one? Are they the same thing? Does the true story have to be beautiful to be believed?

Stories of heroes, monsters, journeys and sacrifice often express our own quest for identity, purpose and deliverance. Narratives can subliminally give comfort by implying that the randomness of our lives maybe doesn't have the final word, but I'm not sure life is made more bearable by in an imaginary god, however beautifully described.

The theologian Frederick Buechner wrote that the gospel was 'a story too good not to be true.' So what makes it good? It's surely not the dazzling language, or easily swallowed wisdom. Even in its most poetic versions it hardly reads like an easy narrative that we might turn to for our entertainment. If you wanted to you could reduce the gospel, even the Bible, to a film executive proof pitch and perhaps describe it as 'the story of a God's relationship with humankind,' but you'd probably have to cut out the convoluted, often repellent bits in between to get it made.

The gospel can be a brutal debunker of human illusion. It's why we tend to keep the bits we like and omit what is difficult. We'd rather turn to other, more pleasing stories, to myths of human progress or pie in the sky fairy tales that are more seductive, but leave us to face the void alone.

It's partly the Bible's unwillingness to please that makes me more inclined to trust it. It is not a neat narrative but a polyphonic, multi-linear anthology, a story that's just too good to be a story. It doesn't try to make us believe in God by asking us to 'imagine' that he is with us, it claims that He actually is with us. That, for me, is surely the better story.

6.12.2012

—

The limits of my kindness

Here's a saying I think few would disagree with: 'Suppose a brother or sister is without clothes and food and one of you says to him, "I wish you well; keep warm and well fed," but does nothing about his physical needs, what good is that?' While the moral logic of this passage from James is perhaps easy to accept, as I discovered this week, practicing it can prove much harder.

On Sunday evening I was walking home from a dinner with my wife. The cold snap had started and with the wind-chill it was about minus five degrees; we were almost home when we saw a man sleeping in the doorway of a shop. We asked if he was okay and he said he was. I was ready to leave him there when my wife asked him if he'd like a bed for the night. He said yes and, seconds later, I found myself carrying his bag back to our house wondering what we were letting ourselves in for.

I'll happily buy a homeless man a cup of tea, a meal, even a sleeping bag but, for all sorts of sensible reasons, offering a bed feels like a line you probably shouldn't cross. As we reached the front door, we told him that we had children and that this was not common practice for us, but we were going to trust him. He said he respected this and so we crossed the threshold.

With our guest tucked up in the spare-room, I must confess that I lay in bed wondering if I should lock the kids' doors or go and hide some of the valuables. I was convinced we'd pay for our naïve, impulsive gesture. The next morning I found everything in its right place. Our guest was asleep on the sofa, and after letting him have a bath (an offer somehow more challenging than offering him a bed) he began to tell us how he'd ended up on the street.

His story was a mix of poor choices and bad luck, regret and self-pity. He was grateful for people's help but was critical of the system. As I listened it confirmed that he needed more than a one-off kindness. Our action would make little difference in the long run. For some reason, the more I found out about him the less sympathetic I felt.

My impatience to get on with my life was more powerful than any desire to help him further and, perhaps unfortunately for both of us, I had found the limits of my kindness.

The rest of that passage from James goes on to say that faith, if not accompanied by action, is dead. Yet it also states that we should do the good we know we ought to do, as the opportunities present themselves. Maybe in the end, it's not our goodness that's the issue; it's our willingness to take a risk. As someone once said, faith is spelt R.I.S.K., it's just not always the kind of risk that can be calculated.

12.3.2013

—

Always on it

A four-year old girl has become the youngest patient to be treated for internet addiction. Psychiatrists said that the child displayed compulsive behaviour after being exposed to the electronic device and symptoms of withdrawal when it was taken away. Apparently, she's being treated through a digital detox.

It's easy to find this story shocking, but I'm pretty sure I need some digital detox. In recent months I've developed a serious dependency on the internet: in particular, a constant need to check messages, to communicate something to someone. Thus far I've done nothing to stop it; like caffeine or violent Nordic crime drama, it's socially acceptable. Like a true addict, I am quick to justify myself: 'It's my job', I say. 'I'm a writer. I need to see how many likes I have. I need to check the ratings. And I have to do it now!' It's a problem. Even my children, who I nag for texting all the time, have noticed it: 'Dad. You're always on it.' Things hit a nadir when, in the middle of family dinner, I found myself checking my messages. When my wife asked me what I was doing, I lied: 'I'm just switching it off'. She fixed me with a look: 'We're trying to have a conversation here.'

Denial, rationalization, delay. I have all the symptoms, but if I went to digital detox, what would they say? They could take away the technological applications, and that would be a start, but would it deal with the root issue? Isn't this technology merely facilitating a pre-existing condition?

Before addiction was a word we used, people talked about attachment. They spoke of our desires becoming enslaved to certain behaviours, things or people. These objects of attachment came to rule our lives. In spiritual terms, the attachment was seen as a form of idolatry, a little false god to which we give our time our energy, even our love. Behind my addiction I suspect there lies a fear: yes, a fear that I won't be heard or read, but a deeper fear that I won't be liked or loved. Meanwhile, I've been putting my faith in the ability of the little gods to tell me what I want to hear.

Christian tradition says that God created us to love Him, but that we usually try to fulfil this deep longing through an attachment to these objects. The initial antidote to this involves a detachment that frees the mind and will to open the heart to greater love. It's not about finding freedom *from* desire (desire being a God given thing); it's about enjoying the freedom *of* desire.

Perhaps if we can accept this grace of God's love and enjoy the liberation it brings, we might no longer need to keep checking to see who likes or loves us. Perhaps then I might even be able to hear and heed the voice speaking to me across the table: 'We're trying to have a conversation here.'

24.4.2013

—

Questions of life and death

Ten years ago in Switzerland some people decided to meet in a café with the express purpose of discussing death. The 'Café mortal' was not, as its name might suggest, a grief support group or end-of-life planning session, but a space where people met to explore death and the questions it raised about life: What is death? How do we live without fearing it? Is death the end? Is there something more? Clearly the founders of the café identified a need because as reported this week there are now death cafés in over 40 cities around the world, including the UK. The movement has a few rules: meetings are confidential and not for profit; everyone must respect other people's views and avoid proselytizing; and coffee and cake are mandatory.

It sometimes seems that society divides neatly into those who claim that death is the end and those who hope that it isn't. In my experience, a lot of people simply haven't had the chance to work out what they think. They're too busy getting on with life, and it's only when death comes to someone we know and love that we give it serious thought.

A few years ago, it became obvious to me that many of my friends weren't interested in going to church. Attempts to encourage them often came with a vague feeling of manipulation. A church, even one trying hard to be welcoming, didn't present them with a comfortable enough space in which to talk about life and its meaning.

Yet I knew from conversations that many of these same friends were up for discussing what philosophers call the first order, or 'Why are we here?' questions. In an attempt to keep the conversation alive, I started a monthly group in a pub. The rituals were simple: we'd meet at 8 o'clock, drink beer for an hour, get through whatever sporting, cultural or political news needed to be got through, and then someone would read a passage of scripture and we'd discuss it. Faith was not a prerequisite, nor was any particular theological knowledge necessary. Just a curiosity and a willingness to talk, listen, think and drink beer. In this pub, the bar was set very low.

The meetings are always different, but they're never dull. There have been disagreements, there have been revelatory moments and, on a couple of occasions, the conversation has gone on long enough to induce a lock-in. Yet apart from the initial oddity of someone reading scripture out loud in a pub, they've come to feel natural and necessary.

It's curious how men will spend hours discussing who should open the batting for England, and yet avoid any chat about what happens when we've played our final innings. After all, as The Book of Job says, 'Death is the meeting house for all mankind'. Of course, there is a time to talk about life, and a time to talk about death; but there should be space somewhere to do both.

26.6.2013

—

The Pope's motor

The Pope's got a new motor; or rather, he's got an old motor, a 1984, Renault 4 GTL with 200,000 miles on the clock. It was given to him this week by a priest who was so inspired by the Pope's call to drive cheap, humble cars and give any remaining money away that he offered the pontiff his car. Pope Francis will shun the luxury limos used to transport previous popes and drive himself around the Vatican in a motor that used to be every French farmers' vehicle of choice. It would be hard to drive a less flashy car or make a clearer statement.

When I got married, we bought an old banger with a rust patch shaped like South America on its side. A neighbour once asked me if the car represented some kind of statement, to which I replied,

'Yeah: my bank statement!' The car was more than adequate transport for relatively impoverished newlyweds, as was our next – a custard yellow hatchback – given to us by people who felt sorry for us driving a car that, by then, had a rust-map of the world on its passenger door.

Of course, cars say something about us. Our values, tastes, income – our stage of life. Now I'm older I feel under more pressure to own something decent, something smarter perhaps than our fifteen-year-old car that my 13-year-old daughter says is an embarrassment. 'Now that's a car,' she says pointing to the sleek, metallic coupé across the road. Of course it's beautiful, and part of me wants it; or maybe that sports car the Swedish detective drove in *The Bridge*. Cars can be lovely things; they can make you feel better about yourself. As Janis Joplin sang, there are fewer more visible statements of status: 'Oh Lord won't you buy me a Mercedes Benz, my friends all have Porsches I must make amends.'

For good or ill, you get judged by what you drive and the Pope knows this. His adoption of the Renault 4 is more than a stunt. Yes, he used to drive one as a priest back in South America and clearly has a soft spot for them; but he also understands society's fixation with status and he wants to subvert it. Driving this car says, 'I'm comfortable with what I've got, I need no extra adornment, and am willing to look un-cool.' Which is the clever part. He makes humility look cool and challenges us to take the same humble road. The car becomes a kind a rolling papal encyclical, a motorized gospel.

The Psalmist wrote, 'Some trust in chariots and some in horses but I trust in the Lord.' If you were looking for a physical expression of this you'd be hard pressed to find a better example than a world leader driving a second-hand, 30 horse power motor car.

17.9.2013

—

Breaking Bad

Drugs have been in the ether this week. A former chief constable has called for the decriminalization of Class-A narcotics to stop millions of pounds going to organized crime. The International Centre for Science in Drug policy declared the 'war on drugs' to be a failure, arguing that drug use be considered a public health issue rather than one of criminal justice. With curiously apt timing, the addictive television series *Breaking Bad*, in which a chemistry teacher becomes a drug dealer, reached its final episode.

Sitting on my sofa with a glass of wine watching a middle-aged man's life escalate into apocalyptic chaos owing to his involvement in the drug world, it's easy to imagine these things are far removed from my comfy, supposedly non-addictive life. Yet part of the show's appeal, as its title suggests, is the way it blurs the border between who is good and who is bad and shows that, at some level, we're all addicts chasing one drug or another. Money, real estate, nicotine, sugar... there's an unlimited supply of addictive substances available and our culture endorses an endless array.

The show dramatizes what the experts are saying, that the law can't keep this beast it bay. There is a deeper issue at work, and it's an issue we can all relate to.

Addiction is defined as a state of obsession or preoccupation that enslaves a person's will and desire. The second letter of Peter puts it this way: 'A man is a slave to whatever has mastered him.'

The psychologist, Gerald May, wrote that, 'To be alive is to be addicted.' It's mankind's natural state. God, he argues, creates us for love and freedom, but we fulfil a longing for him through objects of attachment. These attachments, or addictions, become little gods in which we put our faith. God knows, I have enough of my own, this TV series being one of them. I've had to hide the box-set to stop myself watching during working hours.

Breaking bad habits requires more than will power, another kind of power is needed. Attend any Alcoholics Anonynmous (AA) or

Narcotics Anonymous (NA) meeting and you'll encounter addicts submitting to the help of a higher power, or what they call 'A god of your understanding.' They acknowledge that addiction can't simply be defeated by following rules. Addicts need more than being told to 'just say no!' Discipline is important, but we need the grace of something beyond ourselves and we need it whether we think we deserve it or not.

This is, in essence, a gospel message. For if the law says, 'Good people get good things and bad people get bad,' the gospel says, 'It's the bad that get the best; the worst that inherit the wealth, and the slave who becomes a son.' We're *all* breaking bad, and whether we're watching or not, we are all involved in this great drama – the daily struggle between addiction and grace.

1.10.2013

—

Top of the class

It seems that we're not doing very well in school, again. Out of 65 countries the UK is 26th. Not quite at the back of the class, but no improvement on our position of three years ago. Meanwhile, we're way behind those high fliers, Singapore, Hong Kong and South Korea, whose pupils have once again outshone ours in maths, reading and science. The message seems to be that we must try harder and be more like them if we want to succeed.

While people debate whose fault this is, I wonder if coming top in these tests is a garland we should be striving to win? Yes. We want a productive, rounded and fulfilled generation, but is making children brilliant at passing examinations, whatever the cost, the way to go about it?

Watching a television report on South Korean students, I sincerely doubt it. To make the grade they have to go to school – twice, working with barely a break from 6.30am to 11pm. Their results are exemplary, but they're left too tired to play with friends, hang out or simply just be. 'But look at the success of their economy,' people say. Of course, good education correlates to economic success, but education isn't merely a system for improving GDP. Do we really think, like Dickens's Gradgrind in *Hard Times*, that 'All girls and boys need are facts – nothing else?' I hope not. South Korea has the highest rate of youth suicide in the developed world.

We're such an inventive, creative nation, yet many of the things we're good are hard to measure or forge in an exam room. How many of the Turner Prize contenders would make the PISA grade? How many musicians, novelists or entrepreneurs have an IQ of 130 or above? Indeed, there seems to be a deeper cultural confusion about what intelligence is, limiting it to a measurable IQ while ignoring other qualities such as emotional intelligence.

Surely we need both? This was perfectly illustrated when Lady Ashton helped negotiate a seemingly impossible deal between the US and Iran; it was her 'great emotional intelligence' – her ability to perceive, evaluate and control emotions – that was singled out as making the difference. After all, what's the use of having an intellectually brilliant but socially inept person trying to negotiate a peace treaty between former enemies?

Emotional intelligence is nothing new. Indeed, I'd suggest that it's a form of wisdom. Even the utilitarian Gradgrind wondered if there was 'A wisdom of the head and a wisdom of the heart.' The poor teacher, 'who supposed the head to be all sufficient,' realized too late that it wasn't.

In scripture, wisdom is seen as a synthesis of creative skill, discernment and understanding, as well as a reverence for God. No wonder the author of Proverbs urges us to seek it 'though it cost all we have.' For wisdom, he suggests, is the garland we should want for our children.

4.12.2013

'I only want what's best for my children'

'I only want what's best for my children,' is a common enough sentiment that most parents have thought if not said. Sometimes we bolster the phrase with sacrificial grist: 'I want my children to have what I never had.' This might mean a decent education, a secure home, a holiday in the South of France; whatever it is, our children will have it because we didn't, and we will do everything to make sure they have it... whatever it costs.

Wanting the best for our children seems, on the surface, a perfectly natural and noble aspiration. It's something we hear in the news all the time and it carries a righteous weight. When Jesus asked, 'What parent would give their child a stone when they had asked for bread?' he seemed to be underscoring the fact. What parent wouldn't want their child to have a decent school to go to, clothes that fit, a healthy diet, a home to live in? Yet while it's normal to want these things, he also points out that even the corrupt know how to give their children good gifts. It's easy to prefer your own.

What if what's best for our children is bad for our neighbour's children? I might prefer to ignore this awkward thought, but it manages to insinuate itself in a variety of prosaic ways: particularly in the matter of schooling which, with its scrapping for places, seems to focus self-preferential tendencies more than almost any other area of parental life. However, it goes beyond education: it extends to housing, jobs, community, and it forces us to ask another question: When we want the best for our children, what do we mean by 'the best?'

When asked for guidance about the best way to live this life, Jesus compressed the commandments into an easily learned line about loving God and then our neighbours as ourselves. If the first part is a stretch for someone without faith the latter is at least an ideal people can imagine if not always accomplish. Did he really call us to love our neighbours' kids as much as our own? It might seem completely subversive, but it would be interesting to see what that might do for society.

It's ironic that children – these naturally free, funny, generous rufflers of our best laid plans – have the capacity to turn us into such over-protective reactionaries. If anything they seem, certainly at first, free of this striving insistence on having the best of everything; it's we, the adults, who lay that burden on them. It's as if we start knowing some simple truths, only to forget them later. As it says in Matthew, 'You have hidden these things from the wise and learned, and revealed them to little children.'

When it comes to wanting the best for our kids, let's not limit that aspiration to our own kin.

5.2.2014

—

Right to offend

The recent resignation of a local radio DJ who unwittingly played a song containing an offensive word, highlighted a confusion we have about how we deal with offence in general, and the phrase 'political correctness' in particular.

It's become such a pejorative term. I've not yet met anyone who would gladly describe themselves as politically correct. How often do we hear the phrase, 'It's political correctness gone mad' whenever someone has deliberately (or innocently) said something that might cause offence and is then punished for it? To its detractors it's become a euphemism for some controlling, invisible state apparatus that wants to reduce our every utterance to bland, meaningless nothings.

The phrase was born of good intentions, first used by socialists in the former Soviet Union as a put-down to over-zealous members whose loyalty to the party overrode their compassion for people. It was a mild rebuke with a serious intent. Those same good intentions arguably lay behind an encouragement to use language that minimized social and institutional offence, especially in matters of gender, race, sexual orientation, disability and religious beliefs. (Sorry, if I've I missed anyone there.)

If the term began life as a mild rebuke it's become an easy slur. It's seen as a form of suppressing free speech, used as a standard means of discrediting political enemies or, worse, as a coded cover for those who want to offend people for the sake of it. In fact, it has such shrill, negative associations that maybe it's time to ditch the phrase altogether? Although I'm not sure what would replace it: moral correctness, spiritual correctness, being nice?

The key lies with the word offence. There seems to be a broad consensus about what is offensive in our society. Most of us can agree that offending people – especially the defenceless – for little more than the satisfaction of hurting them is wrong. Yet what if the intention behind an offence is constructive or even corrective? Is it possible that something offensive can be good? Offence can be funny – a host of comedians would have to deliver much shorter sets without it – but as they know it's also a way to subvert prejudice and challenge people's own sense of 'rightness.'

It's tempting to see Jesus as a paragon of political correctness for the way he embraced the marginalized, but he was also the absolute master of the constructively offensive. It's notable that he saved his choicest put-downs for the people who needed to hear them most, i.e. those in power. Yet he wasn't doing this to court popularity and his gauntlet was thrown down for all to pick up. For in the end, this was a man who claimed that a belief in *His* correctness (rather than that of the religious or political establishments) was the true measure of goodness. Words that still sound offensive, even to those who believe them.

13.5.2014

—

A cry for help

Last week I received an email from a colleague who I'd not seen for years. It explained how they'd fallen on hard times and contained a request for a specific amount of money. A follow-up email included bank details and the hope that I might be able to help out; it was much in the style of one of those Nigerian legacy scams. I assumed that their email address had been hacked and so I ignored it. When a further email arrived, explaining a little more and leaving a phone number to call, I began to see it as a genuine if desperate request for help.

Before calling I went through the list of reasons not to help, all sound, all sensible: the money wouldn't be enough to make a difference; they'll just fritter it away; they've got themselves into a hole of their own making; I'm sure I'm not the first person they've asked for help. Yet that same day, with *irritatingly* apt timing, I read the bit of scripture where Jesus says, 'Give to one who asks you, and do not turn away from the one who wants to borrow from you.' When I went back to the text and searched for caveats, I couldn't find any.

All my uming and aghing was rendered academic when I actually spoke to them. They had indeed fallen on hard times: their life had seemed secure: they'd had steady work, a good relationship, a decent flat in a nice part of town – they were probably in that top one per cent that economists talk about. Then they'd fallen off the edge of a cliff. Yes, there were self-inflicted reasons for this plummet – mistakes made, personal demons battled – but the descent to 'living like a dog', as they put it, had been swift. Poverty, as it says in Proverbs, had fallen upon them 'like an armed man.'

As I listened to my colleague's story, the reasons for their descent seemed not to matter so much; it was the 'this-could-be-you-ness' of their plight that struck home. It was much easier to fall off the edge than you'd think, and the thought that it 'could have been me' wasn't just a platitude. Over the course of my life, had I not been on the receiving end of other people's financial help? Had not people's unreasonable generosity got me out of difficulty in the past?

The sheer competitiveness of life, with people seen as winners or losers, the atomizing of community, the widening gulf between rich and poor, makes it seem likely that ever more people will fall off the cliff and not get up again. Yet, as my colleague's story shows, the contingent, fragile nature of life is a reality for all of us. It's a failure of imagination not to be able to picture yourself falling off the edge. We need to be able to picture it because, in the end, the thing that catches someone's fall from grace – is someone else's grace.

23.5.2014

—

Go on, son

I've just seen the film *Boyhood*, a remarkable piece of cinema that charts the development of a boy called Mason from the age of six through to 18. What really makes this coming-of-age movie unique is the fact that it was shot over a period of 12 years, using the same actors. We literally see the cast aging before our eyes and in just a few hours, Mason goes from being a boy playing in the yard on a bike to a man leaving home in his car.

Boyhood is as much about the changing stages of parenthood as it is about growing up. I watched the film with friends who were nearly all parents of children who'd reached the film's inevitable end point. It made for an emotional evening. Mason's mother suddenly being caught out by the realization that her son was finally, actually leaving was a bit too close to home for most of those watching.

I recently saw my own son (just three days shy of his 18th birthday) off on his travels and what should have been a simple summer holiday farewell was freighted with heavier implication and intimation. His journey to life's next stage was well and truly underway. He was setting off a boy and would be coming back a man. The moment caught me out: I knew this day would come, but when it came I was totally blindsided by it. 'Oh boy, he really is leaving home.'

I tried to pull myself together. *This is all good and as it should be. He's a man now. Let him go. Millions of people are going through the same and have been throughout time. Be grateful for the years you've had. Some don't get to enjoy the privilege. Besides, he'll be back and your daughter won't be leaving for a few more years.* None of it was working. By the time I got home I was a heavy-chested wreck. His empty bedroom triggered more waves. From now on, even the mundane would be invested with reminders: no more switching off the left-on light every morning; no more grumbling at the rumble and thrum of band practice. Pretty soon we'd be taking down the blue-tacked posters and choosing paint to make his room into a guest room. Stop!

Seeking solace for this existential wobble I turned to one of the great leaving-home stories – the prodigal son. At first, I wasn't sure if the parallel applied. I'm not expecting my son to fall into a dissolute despond and end up eating pigswill, nor am I expecting him to return home in disgrace. That wasn't the point. The picture of a father letting his son go when he's old enough and then receiving him back unconditionally, with open arms, contains true encouragement for any parent with a child about to leave home: for the love that lets them go is also the love that brings them back.

23. 7. 2014

—

The aftermath

In 1945 my grandfather, a colonel in the British Army, was posted to Germany to help oversee its reconstruction. It was a formidable task. Of the zones, the British was the most devastated. It was said that, 'If the American's got the view, the French the wine, the British got the ruins.' More bombs were dropped on Hamburg in a weekend than on London in three years.

Such was the destruction that the British had to requisition what housing remained in order to accommodate their own families. When my grandfather found a house, he could not face asking the owners to leave; radically, he decided that it was big enough to share. A year on from being enemies, a British and German family were living together under the same roof. They continued to do so for the next five years. Now, 60 years later, those two families are still friends.

I was proud and astonished when my father first told me about this. Apart from showing my grandfather to be an enlightened man, it made me aware of a period of history I knew nothing about. I was expert on the rise of Nazism and the battles of World War Two, but apart from its miraculously quick recovery, I could not begin to tell you what happened to Germany once the war was over.

The current German ambassador, Thomas Mattusek, alluded to this during the V.E. Day celebrations this week, when he suggested that Britain was still obsessed with the Nazi period and ignorant of German history after 1945. For proof you only had to watch the huge amount of programming devoted to Nazi Germany and Hitler. He suggested this emphasis made it difficult for the two nations to really move on from the past.

The trouble is, people are more interested in field marshals than Marshall Plans; war and destruction are more fascinating than peace and reconstruction. They make for more exciting books, films and documentaries. Even, as a 10-year-old boy, growing up 30 years after the war, my favourite comic was *Warlord*, so packed with World War Two action it made me wish the war would never end.

V.E. Day rightly remembers the end of the war and a victory over Nazism, but it also marks the beginning of a period when weapons of war became instruments of peace. The book of Isaiah says that, 'God will judge between the nations, and will settle disputes for many peoples. They will beat their swords into ploughshares and their spears into pruning hooks, Nation will not take up sword against nation, nor will they train for war anymore.'

In 1945, my grandfather and millions of others had to stop being soldiers and retrain to become peacemakers, engineers, educators, builders and administrators. They had to beat their Lee Enfields into typewriters and their tanks into taxis. They conducted a largely hidden, undecorated campaign and yet the peace we now celebrate owes as much to that effort as to the victory that preceded it. It is good to remember the end of a terrible war, but let's not forget those who helped rebuild a lasting peace.

30.7.2014

—

The Fault In Our Stars

The novel *The Fault In Our Stars* is fast becoming a literary phenomenon, attracting millions of readers around the world. John Green's love story about two teenagers with cancer who meet at a support group walks a witty, sometimes brutally frank, line between the potentially sappy and cynical and delivers a profound meditation on the big questions of life.

Its title is a conscious inversion of a quote from Shakespeare's Julius Caesar, where Cassius says to Brutus: 'The fault, dear Brutus, is not in our stars, but in ourselves'. In this face-off between fatalism and self-determinism, Cassius exhorts Brutus to challenge Caesar, insinuating the idea that it's not fate that dooms men, it's their own agency.

Green's title hints at a different world view. Some things (like cancer) clearly have little to do with a failure of personal responsibility. As a former chaplain in a children's hospital, Green would have encountered this reality first hand every day. Interestingly, his experiences with the terminally ill convinced him to become a writer instead of a priest.

He clearly sees that the world is not a wish-granting factory, but a profoundly unjust place where suffering is unfairly distributed and there are severe limitations on our efforts to do anything about it. His novel exposes the sentimental clichés that surround death: 'They've gone to a better place;' 'They will live forever in our hearts.' Yet it isn't a council of despair. His protagonists still live, still love, despite knowing what is coming.

What is coming, of course, is coming for all of us. Which maybe explains why the story hits so deeply for so many. It raises one of the important questions: How do we live honestly and hopefully in the face of the universe's seeming indifference to our suffering and ultimate death? That killer of false dreams, the author of Ecclesiastes, puts it like this: death is the destiny of all men, whether, wise or foolish, healthy or sick. So what is the point?

There is a moment in *Stars* where a character has the feeling that 'The universe wants to be noticed.' Later another character – terrified at the prospect of oblivion – hopes that the universe will notice them. This terror of cosmic abandonment and indifference is directly addressed by Jesus not long before his own death, when he points out that not even a bird falls to the ground without his loving Father knowing it.

The weight of scripture suggests there are no accidents in the universe; it has no time for fatalism or self-determinism. The Psalmist discounts putting trust in the cosmos and knowingly points to the fate of those who (like Cassius) trust only in themselves. It isn't about re-aligning with the distant stars, it's about being re-aligned by the presence of their creator.

4.9.2014

—

'You're not Welsh'

I once went to a six nations game in Cardiff. I needed an extra ticket for a friend. When I found someone with a spare, they said they wanted it to go to a Welshman.

'I am Welsh,' I protested.

'You don't sound Welsh,' he said.

'But I *am* Welsh!'

'Where were you born then?'

'…I was born in Germany, but…'

'Well there you are then!' he said, before asking me where I lived. I admitted I lived in London, but pointed out that I'd grown up in Tenby.

'That's not really Welsh is it?' he said. 'That's Little England beyond Wales.' He then warned the other touts not to sell me a ticket telling them, 'This one's English!'

'Aw, come on!' I said, my accent becoming more Welsh the more agitated I got. 'I'll name the entire Welsh squad for you. I can give you their weights.' It's an acid test of Welshness to be able to guess the weight of tight-head prop Adam Jones, but he'd already found a taker – a man dressed in red, with a proper Welsh accent.

I got into the game with my friend and, happily, Wales beat England, but on the train home to London, surrounded by subdued Englishmen, I had a sense of not belonging anywhere and I found myself wondering how Welsh I really was. I'd been born in a British military hospital in Germany. I'd grown up in Wales, but gone to school and university in England. I'd lived in London for 30 years, married a girl from Essex. I was a passionate Welsh rugby fan, but I supported England at football. I had a Welsh first name, but an English sounding surname. My siblings sounded Welsh to me, I sounded posh to them.

Maybe I was a kind of 'bidoon' – a stateless person found in the Arab peninsula, the descendants of the nomadic Bedouin. Perhaps my nationality wasn't defined by where I lived, but by my attitudes, my loyalties, my beliefs.

It was rugby that gave me a sense of national awareness. Supporting Wales in the 1970s was a source of pride and self-confidence, and the awareness increased when I went to boarding school in England, where I had something to define myself against. When I wrote home, I'd print the address as: house, village, town, county, country, nation, continent, world, solar system and universe – underlining *Wales* in case it went missing.

Maybe the God-like perspective is helpful on this issue of nationality. According to Isaiah, the nations are 'Like a drop in a bucket to Him' and 'He counts the Isles as a very small thing.' At various stages in time, the God of the Bible has revealed Himself to and through individuals, families, tribes and nations. Yet scripture also speaks of people belonging to a different kingdom, a state where there is no distinction between Greek or Roman, Jew or Gentile. *This* is heartening news for the displaced and stateless bidoons of this world.

11.9.2014

—

Act your age

I was half way through an exercise class, trying to do a sit-up on a foam roller, when my friend said very loudly, 'I bet our parents weren't doing this at our age. They'd be at home having a second G&T. The only stretching they did was leaning forward to change the channel to *Poldark* before lighting up a fag.

This, in part, may explain why we are living longer than previous generations and why we keep seeing headlines that tell us that 40 is the new 30, 90 the new 70 and, most recently, 50 the new 20. This last off the back of a survey done for *High 50* magazine claims that 40 per cent of the over fifties are having sex twice a week and a 'sizeable minority' are taking recreational drugs.

Having just turned 50, I'm excited by these recalibrations of my age, but no amount of spin can change the fact that, if 30 felt like the end of youth and 40 passed with barely a nod, 50 feels like a proper, grown-up age. Whatever magazines might be telling me, the body I'm waking up with the day after five-a-side football is saying, 'You're 50. Get used to it.'

So why not get used to it? Maybe it's partly because our culture sees so little merit in getting older. This constant re-branding of each decade is as much about disguising age as about celebrating it. We're dressing it up in youth's apparel because we believe young is better than old. Old must be delayed, avoided, renamed.

I don't expect to live long enough to see the headline '20 is the new 50!' but there are things I know now that I'd liked to have known then. Being older has its advantages, and in another culture and age it didn't have to mimic youth to claim validity. In the Old Testament experience was valued so highly that 50-year-olds were allowed to retire from certain physical duties so that the community could make the most of their accumulated wisdom.

As a boy, my elders were often telling me to be thankful, but I've almost had to get to *their* age to appreciate what they wanted me to thankful for. At recent parties celebrating the landmarks of 50 and 60, there has been a real sense of gratitude: for making it this far, for friendships, for family, for life. Maybe that gratitude is a kind of understanding. It's why the Psalmist asks, 'Teach us to number our days so that we might gain a heart of wisdom.'

Scripture says life might last 70 years, 80 if we have the strength, but it doesn't pretend this span won't have troubles or sorrows. It seems we have a choice between living out whatever days we have by raging at our aging and pretending that it isn't really happening, or being glad for what we have and celebrating it as we can – with gratitude, and as much dancing as our bodies can take.

25.11.2014

The great protagonist

How do you tell a story that has a largely invisible protagonist? How do you make plausible a character who is beyond our powers of description, one who is utterly alien to us? Making God believable is a particular challenge for the visual arts and perhaps a reason why so many films inspired by the biblical narrative have such a hard time personifying the One who lies at its heart.

Despite the technical (and aesthetic) challenges, God is back once again in 72 mm 3D surround-sound, this time appearing (if that's the word) in a retelling of the Moses story. It's the turn of the mighty Ridley Scott (no stranger to the alien) to give us his interpretation in the new film *Exodus: Gods and Kings*. Like all those who came before him, Scott has had to deal with the problem of God. Does he face him full on as Moses did on Mount Sinai, or does he explain him away through knowable phenomena?

In a less literal-averse age, Cecil B. de Mille had God's voice booming from behind a bush in his *Ten Commandments*; Scott has God appearing to Moses as a boy and speaking in a still small voice, and while viewers are free to attribute Moses's visions to a head injury or give a scientific explanation to the intellectually embarrassing parting of the Red Sea, the film seems not to duck the source material.

Thank God we live in a time and a culture where people are free to tell and interpret these stories for themselves. It's interesting that, thousands of years later, they're still being told. Of course, for some the story of Moses is more than a ripping yarn, it's a vital part of a greater whole, a sort of Part One in an epic that starts with a God who creates, continues with a God who reveals himself to a people and reaches a fulfilment with this God stepping onto the stage himself.

This part of the story, the Incarnation, will be told and re-told throughout this advent week, as the Bible supplies its own three-dimensional version of the elusive and mysterious God that features in its earlier chapters. The part of the story where God becomes man is perhaps the most fantastic, intellectually challenging part of all. The writer Dorothy Sayers once wrote, 'How strange, how interesting the narrative is. It really is a sensational story, more sensational than anything else. Imagine for a moment it being put in the papers!'

As Sayers recognized, the story is only sensational if it is historical, more than a myth or a general truth. An event involving a living person who some interpret as being the incarnation of God. A story still worthy of being re-told and re-imagined for people seeking the Great Protagonist in their own story.

2.12.2014

—

The finger of God

The Hubble Telescope was launched by NASA 25 years ago and sent out to gather images of the distant stars and galaxies of *our* universe, and perhaps someone else's universe, too. It has delivered some of the most beautiful and memorable images of our time – of all time, from all time. When the front page of a newspaper carries a picture of the latest discovery of a nebula, or triple-moon conjunction, or loopy galaxy, the chances are it will have been taken by the Hubble.

One shot in particular, taken in 2010, sticks in the mind. It shows the Carina Nebula, a pillar of cloud three light-years tall, with stars being born in the gas and dust. Its nickname is 'The Finger Of God'. When I first saw it I experienced a constellation of reactions: 'Wow! What is that? Woe is me!' You could say I had been totally 'Hubbled', which I'd loosely define as the state of wonder induced by seeing images from the Hubble telescope.

This brilliant machine has done what it was designed to do, but as well as gathering hard scientific data, it's done something else: it's provoked wonder, fired people's imaginations, got them thinking about their place in the universe. The fascinating thing is that, like some Cosmic Rorschach Test, people conclude different things from what they see.

One person sees these images as a perfect demonstration of human insignificance. Proof that we are, as Douglas Adams put it, 'The denizens of a small planet in the un-chartered backwaters of the unfashionable end of the western spiral arm of the galaxy.' While another thinks, 'So, in all this infinite chaos, where there are black holes and dead ice planets, I happen to be on the one with the exact conditions required to sustain life. Not only that, I get to question that life and look back at other planets in search of answers.'

Whatever our world- or planet-view, I'm not sure there's a correct reaction. Wonder can't be prescribed. We are free to feel our total insignificance, just as we are free to find significance. We can feel both if we want. I trust and need the scientists to tell me that the cloud of gas is made of hydrogen and that it's three light-years high, but I can still feel a numinous glory and connection as much a cosmic terror and isolation.

Trying to understand our place in the universe is as much a part of the faith journey as it is the scientific. Questions of significance and insignificance lie at the heart of the Psalmist's question to God: 'When I consider your heavens and the work of your fingers, the moons and the stars, what is man that you care for him?'

In an age where it is hard to see religion and science in the same space, the Hubble telescope has provided beautiful and unexpected perspective.

4.3.2015

—

Crowd mentality

On Saturday, I was at Loftus Road watching Queens Park Rangers play Tottenham. The fact it was a London derby and that QPR badly needed a result gave the game added spice. The chanting of the home fans started humorously enough. They declared their footballing supremacy in both West London and the world; the superiority of their striker, Charlie Austin, their low regard for all things Chelsea. They even generously offered to sing a song for the visiting fans in the absence of any audible support. It was vigorous and funny.

Then Tottenham scored and the object of the chanting moved from ribbing the opposition fans to questioning the visual capacity and impartiality of the referee. All standard fan-banter, but when Tottenham scored again, wit was totally abandoned in favour of hurling rank abuse at the match officials and the players. The ugly mood reached a nadir when a fan next to me screamed anti-semitic abuse at a Tottenham player, a club with strong Jewish associations.

Impressively, this last insult drew an immediate reaction from someone behind us who told him to sit down and leave it out, which mercifully he did. Around the ground, hoardings displayed the logos of the *Kick It Out* campaign, an organization committed to getting rid of all forms of discrimination in football and, no doubt, they'd have been heartened by this example of an individual standing up to racial abuse.

Although why stop there? What about the abuse that sees a linesman being called unrepeatable things for 20 minutes by a man leading a choir of a thousand people? Some will say that's part of the game. I'm sure most fans who dish out the verbals know where to draw the line, but for much of this match I wasn't quite sure where that line was.

A crowd is an intoxicating thing. I admit to the giddy pleasure of being swept up in the passion and partisanship, the tribal sense of belonging. Yet there's anonymity and safety in crowds that can encourage people to hide, to sublimate their own morality to the will of the group. We then become stupefied by the power of others and by our own powerlessness in the face of it.

'Do not follow the crowd into doing wrong,' scripture warns. The Psalmist even asks to be hidden from the noisy crowd that 'Sharpen their tongues like swords and aim their words like arrows, shoot at the innocent man,' while encouraging each other in the knowledge that in a crowd no one will know it's them.

I went to watch a game of football, but ended up experiencing a strange mix of entertainment, abuse and faint menace, as well as having to face my own moral cowardice. Thankfully, someone was courageous enough to do what I couldn't and take a stand. As football fans themselves prove, it only takes one person to change the chant of the whole crowd.

10.3.2015

—

What is love?

It's the most searched for phrase on Google and was a hit record for dance act Haddaway in the early 1990s. Now, a team of scientists from China and the US have been attempting to find some answers to one of humanity's most enduring questions: What is love?

Using MRI scans to track the physical effects of love on the brain, researchers monitored three groups of students: those who were 'in love', those who had recently ended relationships and those who had never been in love. The study claims to have successfully obtained evidence of alterations in brain function, with those 'in love' showing increased brain activity especially in the parts that deal with emotion regulation and social cognition.

It could be claimed the data demonstrates the power of love to change us, but does an observable increase of serotonin, pheromones and dopamine tell us more about love than, say, the song 'Love is the Drug?' In fact, if you want to know what love is, you could ask a musician. Since the charts began, 60 per cent of the top ten hits have been about love and it's been variously described as 'all you need, blind, a crazy little thing', and 'deeper than a river and higher than a mountain.'

Love it seems needs more than one word to define it. The Greeks helpfully supplied a few: giving us *philia* to describe the intimacy between friends; *agape* for a selfless kind of love, and *eros* to describe romantic sexual love. While it's probably the latter that keeps rock stars in royalty cheques and even scientists conducting brain scans, there are clearly other kinds of love worth singing about as well as analysing.

Back in the 1980s, the writer Scott Peck made a distinction between being 'in love' and 'love', describing 'in love' as a feeling that is spontaneous, effortless and temporary, while 'love' involved an action that was deliberate, demanding and lasting. It's much more than a passing feeling: it involves commitment, a steadiness, 'an ever fix-ed mark that looks on tempests and is never shaken.'

The philosophers, poets and prophets have all been nudging us closer to a fuller, more mature understanding of what Love might be. Yet even among the most eloquent, there is no single description that covers it, just as for science there is no irreducible formula. Nothing we can locate, put under a microscope and say 'Eureka, I've found love!'

Perhaps the scientists are measuring the wrong thing. Maybe the real evidence of love's activity can't be scanned. For it's found in the millions of hidden actions of giving and receiving that take place between people every day. The commandment 'Love God with all your heart, mind and soul and your neighbour as yourself' makes no sense without somebody to love and the somebody who loves. Love needs bodies to make it incarnate, and it has to be incarnate to be Love.

17.3.2015

Love your neighbour, even if they voted for the wrong party

For the last few weeks I've been breaking the taboo that says you should never discuss politics or religion at dinner by directly asking friends and neighbours who they're voting for, whether they're going to vote, and why.

The experiment has reminded me of a couple of important truths: first, that people we really like sometimes have completely different political convictions to us (over half the friends I talked to will not be voting the same way as me tomorrow); second, that we can only go so far when impressing our opinions on others.

Being opinionated, I did my best to make my friends see things my way. The conversations have been enjoyable and sometimes feisty. It was only when a note of absolute certainty entered the discussion that it polarized, fizzled out and we went back to discussing *Game of Thrones* or the relegation battle.

For the most part, people are perfectly capable of holding in tension the fact that while politics can be a vital means of improving lives it can't make everything better. It is perfectly normal to think that the party you're voting for is the best of the bunch while recognizing they may not be up to the task.

Some might see this as cynicism. I'd suggest it's more a healthy scepticism. Churchill recognized it when he said, 'Many forms of Government will be tried in this world of sin and woe. No one pretends that democracy is perfect or all-wise. It's the worst form of government except for all those other forms that have been tried!'

On a radio show yesterday a man was asked how the outcome of the election would affect him and he said he'd still have to get up in the morning and do his best to get through the day. It wasn't a political criticism, more an existential reality. There are aspects of life not covered by the party manifesto and nor should they be.

It's a sign of a healthy society that it is prepared to accept that politics should go just so far and no further. It is the wisdom of democracy that it doesn't try to politicize the whole of society's life, even allowing people to defer to other powers. A distinction Jesus alluded to when he told us to render to Caesar what is Caesar's and to God what is God's.

Of course, in some countries political differences threaten life itself. Spare a thought for the people of Burundi. As the world's third poorest nation enters elections, 40,000 people have fled the country because they are refusing to vote as they've been ordered to by the ruling party's militia. That's a high price to pay to have a say.

Thank God we are free to have our say at the polling booth tomorrow without threat of violence or coercion. The outcome may be uncertain, but when the result comes we should at least be able to live in peace with it, and get back to the challenge of loving neighbours who sometimes don't vote the way we do.

6.5.2015

—

Who will buy the son?

The record for a work of art sold at auction was broken yesterday at Christie's in New York. When auctioneer Jussi Pykannen brought his gavel down on the bidding for Picasso's *Women of Algiers*, the final amount was £102 million. The painting was described by one executive as the most exciting to come on the market in ten years and 'a big show-off picture.' He added that in another ten years £102 million would seem inexpensive.

He's probably right. Ten years ago, when a Picasso was sold for just over £50 million, everyone said the market had peaked... and here we are. It's not unlike the prices paid for football players, it seems futile to complain. In this world something is always worth what someone else is willing to pay for it. Of course, it's not just about the art, it's about the investment. These high prices have as much to do with low interest rates as aesthetics. A fine painting can bring pleasure to its owner; an expensive one can bring them a return.

I know a brilliant artist who doesn't quite make a living from the sale of his paintings, even though, to my eye, he should. Not so long ago it was suggested to him by the owner of a gallery that if he wanted to be taken more seriously, he should put the prices of his pictures up – by ten times! People would see more in them if they were more expensive.

Which brings me to an apocryphal story about a rich man who enjoyed collecting art. His many homes were full of Cezannes and Picassos. One day his son was killed in action after saving another man's life. Months later the man whose life had been saved came to see the father, bringing with him a portrait he'd painted of the son. 'It's not great art,' he said, 'but I thought you might like it.'

A few years later, when the rich man died, all his artworks went to auction. The auction began with the picture of the son. The connoisseurs complained that it didn't constitute real art and when the auctioneer asked for bids, nobody responded. He asked again: 'The son? Who will take the son?' Eventually a frail gentleman, the deceased man's gardener, offered $10. It was all he had, but nobody raised the bid, so it was his.

Suddenly, the auctioneer brought down his gavel and declared the auction over. There was an uproar. What about the real paintings? It was then that the auctioneer made known the rich man's will. He'd stipulated that the person who bought the portrait of his son would inherit the entire estate, including the Picassos. The art collector had recalibrated the value system. The man who got the son got everything.

It's a parable that could have come from a gospel. For beyond the bang of the gavel, there is another beauty to be found. One that's rooted in love and relationship, and always open to the lowest bidder.

13.5.2015

Sheen Sundays

A few years ago I stopped going to church on Sunday mornings, partly because I wanted to play football with a group of local dads. The team are collectively known as 'Sheen Sunday' and they display an inclusiveness – a social, ethnic and religious mix – you'd struggle to find in some congregations. It included an electrician, a musician, a builder, a neuro-surgeon, a shopkeeper and a comedian; Iranians, a Pole, Albanians, a Canadian, a Muslim, a Jew, a Bahai, resolute atheists, a lot of don't knows and a few don't cares. Because some are now old enough for our sons to play, the ages run from 15 to 63.

However, with news that researchers at the London School of Economics have discovered that practising a religion is better for mental health than sport, I wonder if I've made the wrong choice; that I might be jeopardizing my long-term happiness if not my mortal soul. Their research showed that religious activity (defined here as going to church, mosque or synagogue regularly) played an important role in keeping depression at bay and providing a coping mechanism during periods of illness. The study couldn't prove how much this was down to faith in a God or the sense of belonging that comes from being part of a group, but concluded that it furnished people with a sense of purpose, identity and security.

Of course, playing football can give people a sense of belonging, purpose and even joy that for some counts as religious activity. Indeed, one of the dads recently said to me that the football was his church. The team may not be gathering to play and celebrate the reconciliation of the world which has taken place in Jesus Christ, but he had a point: both football and church require organization, money for the meeting, a regular time and place to meet and a few agreed rules. Both are communities dependent on meaningful relationships to support the activity.

There was a time when a faithful follower of Christ might be expected do 'an Eric Liddle' and refuse to play sport on the Sabbath. I wonder if today 'religious activity' can be limited to a particular day or even place. Jesus himself said, 'Men and women weren't made for the Sabbath. The Sabbath was made for men and women.' Implying that our worship – if we want to give it – is more important than the where and the when.

Playing football instead of going to church isn't a clash of faith and unbelief, it's just a clash of timetables. Nor is it, for all its unexpected similarities, a substitute. The church carries a great hope beyond itself, and that hope continues to draw some to pursue God with others, even if not always at the usual time. Perhaps when researchers are trying to analyse religious activity or quantify how many people are worshipping God, they'd do well to look outside as well as in the regular places of worship, even to the playing fields beyond.

8.9.2015

—

Stents and statins

As my doctor's appointment overruns by 20 minutes my sense of entitlement rises with my blood pressure. The packed waiting room is grumbling too and it is easy to see why representatives of 7,000 GPs are claiming that they cannot cope with the existing demands of their patients.

My doctor apologizes for the wait and during the consultation I ask how he is coping. He suggests it's a constant challenge trying to meet everyone's needs and expectations. 'The thing is,' he says, 'I never know what's coming through the door. It could be a sore throat. It could be a cancer. Either way it's a person, but ten minutes often isn't enough to give the patient what they need.'

It's disconcerting to think of doctors not having the time to provide the care they would like. The traditional image of the GP is a figure of unruffled authority, dispensing calm certainties and healing. Part of the problem lies not just with increased numbers of patients, but in the fact that medical advances are prolonging life. In this age of stents and statins, people are living longer and thus more are experiencing diseases of aging that require further medical support.

Doctors have always inhabited the frontier of life and death, a place where duties and rights collide and difficult choices have to be made: whether to dispense costly drugs, whether to up a treatment or stop it altogether; how to balance optimism with realism while trying to remain human in the brief window they have with their patient. All the while holding in tension the reality that we are – as T. S. Eliot brutally put it – all dying.

In his great poem *The Wasteland*, Eliot wrote, 'He who is living is now dead, we who were living are now dying, with a little patience.' It's interesting that the word patience shares the same root as the word we give to someone receiving medical care, particularly when patience is hard to find in a world where people expect their doctor to make them better.

Significantly, both words come from the Latin for suffering, from which we get the word passion. In those lines from *The Wasteland*, Eliot was referring to The Passion of the Christ, where another clash of duty and rights occurs. The raising of blood pressure in Gethsemane may have had cosmic implications, but the questions Jesus puts to God are the questions most patients put to their doctors: Can you make it better? Can you stop this suffering? How can I control this finitude?

When a prophet once said we are not promised tomorrow, it wasn't to leave us in despair, but to urge us to lose one kind of life to embrace another. Maybe letting go of the illusion that we can control our own atrophy and mortality is part of the salve that we seek.

15.9.2015

Amy sings the blues

My local pub has a chalkboard outside on which the landlord writes a different quote every week. This week's quote is from Amy Winehouse and it says, 'Every bad situation is a blues song waiting to happen.' This great singer, who died at the age of 27 from alcohol poisoning, is the subject of a new documentary, a painful and powerful study of a towering talent brought low, for the most part, by the earthquake of fame.

With her extravagant licks of eyeliner and beehive hair, and her humiliating public fall, there was something so cartoonish about the Amy Winehouse persona that it was easy to forget there was a person there. Using intimate footage, this documentary succeeds in showing you a person – a mouthy, beguiling, very funny girl, but one with normal worries about spots and weight and boyfriends. An ordinary North London Jewish girl who happened to be blessed with a world-class talent. When we first hear it, as she sings happy birthday aged 14, the voice is so incredible you wonder if it's really coming from her. It seems transcendent, a divine gift.

Such a talent had to rise and there is a thrill in seeing her gain a record deal and then recognition. Even though we know what's coming and see the flaws (an attraction for weak men, an addictive personality) that will crack and break her later, we still will her to make it. We almost don't hear it when she suggests, long before the tidal wave of fame hits her, that she won't be able to handle it. Much later, she will say, 'If I could give it all back just to walk down that street with no hassle – I would', but by then it's too late.

If fame is the condition of being known, usually on account of a notable achievement, it seems that it actually leads to a state that is its very opposite. Being renowned is not being known at all. Fame with its empty chatter, easy confessions, senseless compliments and boring confidentialities, dehumanizes people on both sides of the equation; it even requires us to de-personalize the famous so that we can feel we own them; so we can shout out their names, reduce them to an image, make them a thing.

In the lyrics of this North London Jewish girl it's possible to detect a spiritual ancestry in the Psalmist. He would use 'the bad situations in life' to sing of his woes to the one he believed truly knew him. She may have sung about rehab and lamented treacherous lovers, but her addictions contained the same craving for a deeper rehabilitation, and a better definition of personhood. I think she would have appreciated the Psalmist's song: 'O lord you know me and even before a word is on my tongue you know it completely.' For in the cries of both these singers we hear the desire to be truly known.

15.9.2015

—

Not for sissies

It's no surprise that there's been such a heartfelt response to the interview with 83-year old Sally Lebanov after she talked with great dignity and stoicism about the nature of her home care visits. 'They used to be half an hour,' she said, 'but by the time the care visitor had booked in and out (most aren't paid until they've booked in) there was usually only ten minutes left.' Time enough perhaps to choose between having her commode emptied or hot water bottle filled – but not both. She had not had a bath for three years.

Her situation might have been exacerbated by cuts to public services, but, as she pointed out, it wasn't just about money. This remarkably uncomplaining woman admitted that while she would like to have some basic physical needs met – her legs exercised, her toenails cut, her bed changed more often – what she really wanted was time to have a meal with her visitor. Even just a chat or maybe a trip to the shops. She was lonely, she said, and missed the companionship of others. She wanted company as much as care – the kind of care that can't be always be legislated for.

I like the sound of Mrs Labanov, but I'm not sure I like the sound of old age. Bette Davies memorably said old age wasn't for sissies. In general, it's seen as a negative experience, commonly described as a burden. Mrs Labanov herself joked about being in God's waiting room and, although she vividly gives the lie to this picture, it sometimes seems that society sees waiting to die as the main purpose of life's final stage. Despite there being many good carers doing the best they can, we continue to see failings in meeting the needs of the elderly.

Perhaps this failure is connected to the difficulty we have – unless we've already got there – in imagining what it is to be old. To care-free youth, old age is something that only comes to – well – old people. The old inhabit another country. While the middle-aged, with their increasing intimations of what lies ahead, would rather not think about it, preferring to deny its inevitability. Both attitudes can deafen us to the needs of the old, even blind us to the fact they exist.

When the Psalmist cried out to God, 'Do not cast me off in old age,' he was afraid of being left alone. God didn't promise to stop the aging process, but he did promise to be with him in his last days. He encourages us to respect the old for their wisdom and experience; and asks that we give them our care, time and love. Most of us will be old ourselves one day, which is why it's so important to listen to the voices of those who've already got there.

21.11.2015

—

The house that fell down

There was once a house in a big city that fell to the ground with a great crash. Fortunately, no-one was hurt; the owner wasn't home and the builders working at the site escaped injury.

The collapsed house was a shocking sight: the front of the building had come away like a doll's house, revealing the flimsy rooms inside. People asked, 'How could something so well made just fall down?' At first it was sad and disconcerting, but when they heard the house had collapsed because the owner, a millionaire not even in the country, had been building a cinema in his basement, they no longer felt sympathy. Instead they said, 'It serves them right.'

Eventually the fallen house had to be razed. The people who walked past it on their way to work looked upon the rubble as a sort of visual parable, a 'told-you-so' of biblical proportions. Throughout the neighbourhood you could hear the smug hum of Schädenfreude.

Soon, the collapse of the rich person's house became a symbol of what was wrong with the housing situation in the big city – a place where some struggled to afford a home at all, while others hollowed out their already burgeoning spaces in search of even more. While some went to bed at night, free of the need (or the means) to put a cinema in their basement, others felt unsettled. If this event had been an object lesson, what was it teaching them? Was it enough just to feel pleasure at a wealthy person's come-uppance?

One night, a man who lived close to the fallen house felt his own house vibrating as the train went past. It made him wonder: Could his own house come tumbling down? How deep and secure were its foundations? To calm his nerves, he remembered an old story about one man who built his house on rock and another who built his on sand, and how the one built on rock survived the storms of life. He knew this story was not about architectural engineering and he wondered: What was that rock and have I built my house on it?

Searching the scriptures, he found the story and saw that it was a parable told by Jesus just after he had delivered his Sermon on the Mount. The man who built his house on the rock was anyone who heard the words of Jesus and put them into practice. Yet the man still wondered: which words did he mean? He looked again, and saw that the words were about healing the sick, feeding the hungry, loving people you didn't like, and not judging anyone in case the thing you wanted to happen to them happened to you. With that he closed the book and started to think again about the foundations upon which his house was built.

29.1.2016

—

Hymns, arias and anthems

It's the start of the Six Nations rugby tournament and throughout these lands people will be digging out their team colours, dusting off their sense of national identity and arguing about who's got the best chance of winning (Wales, of course). For rugby fans the Six Nations is part of the rhythm of the year, getting them through the short, dull days of late winter, the banter between fans generating a bit of extra heat at weekends. The singing of your country's anthem, as though your life depends upon it, getting the blood and passions flowing.

Some think that a well-sung anthem is worth a seven-point head-start to the home side. When I was growing up this was more like 14 points if you were Welsh, because they already had the best anthem, the best singers and, back then, the best players playing in the best stadium. That was before they put in a retractable roof so that God could watch. That said, being an English-speaking Welsh boy, I had to learn the anthem using the memory prompt of 'A hen laid a haddock on oily old me.' An image that has, over the years, reinforced my belief that anthems are both wonderful and absurd.

Indeed, all six of the anthems sung this weekend contain elements of the sublime and the ridiculous. They are by turns sentimental, militaristic, hubristic, fanciful and downright cut-throat. The Welsh anthem claims we are 'a land of poets and singers' (fair dos) but 'a people of great stature'? That's a stretch, unless you're Alun-Wyn Jones. The Scots sing a song, composed in 1967, about sending an invader homeward to think again, that invader being the English army in 1314. The brilliant but unhinged French anthem has pedigree, but don't dwell too long on the sentiments. The Irish, admirably seeking to cross national lines, sing an anthem that sounds like it was hastily composed in a pub. Meanwhile, some English, claiming they don't have their own anthem because they have to share it with the rest of the UK, want to replace 'God Save the Queen' with 'Jerusalem'.

No matter. Nae bother. De rien. Non importa! If the English want to sing Jerusalem, let them. It's got a banging tune by Parry and great words by Blake. No one will mind that this piece of Christian eschatology both satirizes English nationalism – indeed all nationalism – while envisaging a future where national boundaries no longer matter. It's a spiritual vision that's worth hoping for.

However, while we wait for the fulfilment of this ideal, it's fine – and healthy – to sing an anthem wholeheartedly while secretly thinking it a load of twaddle. Or praise your nation's virtues while knowing its limitations. These anthems are glorious bits of cheerleading, not war cries. They prove a shared heritage as much as nationalistic difference and I'd argue that most people singing their anthems so fervently this weekend already know this.

As for the rugby: feed me till I want no more.

6.2.2016

—

Mother should know

A study from YouGov shows that the number of parents who would be upset if their children married or partnered with someone of a different political persuasion has doubled in the last eight years.

I'm not sure if this shows that politics is becoming more polarized or parents becoming less tolerant, but you'd think most parents would be pleased that their children had any political convictions, such is the low level of political engagement being shown by the young across the democratic world. Yet children having different beliefs to their parents is surely the way it's always been? I have different political convictions to my mother, I have differing theological views to those of my father, while my children are still questioning how relevant either of these things are. Do I love them less; do we stop discussing it? Lord, I hope not.

Of course, Mum knows best – until you disagree with her. I'd be curious to know how the Prime Minister really feels about his mother signing a petition this week, against local government cuts to children's centres in her son's constituency. I find it oddly reassuring that she did; it's better to be part of a family, or a society, that is able to hold difference or indifference in tension while continuing to care for one another. There's nothing creepier than kids blindly agreeing to everything their parents think or parents praising everything their children do.

There is a concept in political theory known as The Overton Window, which is the spectrum of ideas that the public find acceptable. It's the window in which politicians operate. However, politicians, like parents, need to keep up with changing ideas, and the fact is that the window can move, or get smashed altogether. An idea that was once deemed unthinkable (such as same sex marriage, or universal free health care at the point of need) can, in the skip of a generation, become policy. Yesterday's radical is today's reasonable.

In their children, parents have to face what politicians of all persuasions have to face: a shifting set of beliefs that challenges their view of the world and how it should be run. As a parent, you can spend years nurturing and influencing your children, training them in the way you think they should go, and all of sudden they turn to you and say, 'I don't agree with you.' It might be upsetting, but shouldn't we also welcome the challenge?

When scripture encourages children to honour their mother and father that doesn't mean believing everything they believe. It means loving them despite what they believe, and when it urges parents not to provoke or exasperate their children, it's asking them to respect their fledgling thoughts and remember that they sometimes see the world through a different window. In this life, some things are even more important than the preservation of our convictions.

12.2.2016

—

I'm worth it

When the writer of Luke's Gospel says, 'A worker deserves their wages,' he doesn't make a distinction between different types of work, and doesn't give us clues as to the size of the pay packet. He merely leaves us with the pragmatic wisdom that if you do the work you get paid. Few people I know would dispute that.

Many workers, no matter what they do, would also say they're worth every penny they're paid (perhaps more). This too is a commonly expressed belief that's hard to challenge, but a new book by economist Robert Frank makes the observation that the more successful a person the more keenly they feel a sense of being worth every penny, and the less likely they are to attribute their success to other factors, such as birth or environment, or that arbitrary force some call luck.

This inclination is demonstrated in the Cookie Monster Experiment conducted by psychologists at Berkeley University, in which they divide people into groups of three and arbitrarily appoint a leader. The group is given a task and half way through a surprise plate of cookies is put on the table. Everyone takes a cookie but there is always one left. In over half the cases the randomly appointed leader takes the last cookie. Why? Because they deserve it of course.

Thinking we deserve the extra cookie because of our own merits and ignoring the other things that got us there goes deep. A successful film producer once said, 'The harder I work the luckier I get,' pointing to the reasonable connection between effort and reward; but what happens when we work hard, have all the skills, and we don't get the reward? Is it just a case of 'tough cookie?'

When a person attributes their success solely to their own efforts it can be problematic for them as well as others. First, it's a kind of delusion. Anyone who has experienced success has someone else to thank: their colleagues, the stars, their God. When Lenny Henry spoke to some prisoners recently, he was quick to thank his mum. He himself had been a clipped ear away from a life behind bars. This 'but-for-the-grace-of-God' gratitude is important for it both debunks the self-made delusion while giving us a more realistic measure of our worth.

In a winner-takes-all, I'm-worth-it society, perhaps grace is a more generous and secure thing to live by than luck. Where luck really is random and impersonal, grace is purposeful and relational. Grace initiates but doesn't dominate. It has room for the hard-working success story as well as the hard-working failure, and it shows us the fine, almost invisible, line between them. Knowing that our good fortune – or our worth – comes from something other than just our own efforts probably makes us more inclined to share the cookies.

29.4.2016

—

Oh God, help

It is said that in times of great uncertainty people pray more, so we can assume the lines are jammed right now. With a recent report, from the think-tank Theos, suggesting that praying together is good for us whether we believe prayer 'works' or not, maybe we should all be looking for somewhere to pray and someone to pray with?

Twenty years ago, a friend of mine started a prayer group that met every Friday in his garden shed. Over the years the sheds and heads have changed, but the group still meets. In 20 years you end up praying through a lot of wars, government collapses, stock market crashes and England football fiascos. Were all our prayers for peace and stability answered? Clearly not. Did we carry on praying? Yes. Twenty years has also seen a lot of prayers for help and healing shot out from sheds, front rooms and allotments; was every single request met? Not really. There was a man we prayed for who came out of a coma, but there was also the mother of two who didn't come through the cancer. Did we give up praying after that? Of course not.

In its widest sense, prayer is a universal human activity, as elemental as breathing. For some it springs from a yearning far deeper than simply needing to get stuff we want. We know (unless we're deluded) that we can never completely control our personal lives or events in the world. We thus bridge the gap between what we can do and what is done to us by wishing, longing, despairing and hoping. All of these can be forms of prayer.

We might pray because we are grateful or we might pray because we are desperate, but we still pray. As Abraham Lincoln said, 'I'm driven to my knees by the overwhelming conviction that I have nowhere else to go.' At its most basic, we utter prayers in the hope that there is something good underpinning all of life, something at the core of existence that can bring stability to our wobbly lives in this volatile world.

These prayers don't have to be long or eloquent and maybe don't even require great faith. My friend's preferred prayers were usually 'Oh God, help!' and 'Jesus, please do something!' Jesus himself said the shorter our prayers the better. When the disciples asked him how to pray, he gave them the Lord's Prayer, one of pithiest mixes of poetry and practicality ever uttered. Be thankful, be direct and bring your requests, but do it all with a confidence and hope that prayers, whether offered up from sheds or cars, cathedrals or beds, do not go out and come back void, but are heard by a God who is a very present help in times of trouble.

29.6.2016

—

Death by news

The radio is on in the background and they're talking about a leadership election getting ugly and you half listen because it's not an unimportant event, but you still haven't finished digesting the digested versions of Chilcott's 2.6 million words, to try and understand what was what and who to blame; but there's another leadership contest being announced, plus a big article about racial problems in America to read, and you ought to watch the interview with the person who might be the next prime minister; so you do that while sifting through all the tweets and posts about Brexit, and after a while you feel you've absorbed a lot of information but learned nothing, and you feel angry or anxious or confused; so instead you watch Murray win Wimbledon or the entire season five of *The Walking Dead* and let the consolations of sport or the fictional problems of a post-apocalyptic world take your mind off it all.

There have been times these last few weeks when it's been hard to keep up with the news – even in barest outline. The speed, the momentousness, the clamour of it, and the short amount of time we have to process – let alone understand – it all increases a sense of feeling overwhelmed. Someone recently asked, 'Is Britain about to die of news?' It's even been suggested the news is bad for us; that rather than informing us, it inhibits thinking, makes us passive and indifferent to the suffering of others, while re-affirming us in our existing prejudices. Add to that the problem of the news itself being distorted or mis-reported and it's tempting to ignore it all – for good.

I'm not sure withdrawal is the answer. It's often when events are at their most confusing and troubling that we need to engage in order to understand them better. The challenge for us seems to be: how do we stay informed about the issues of the day without being overwhelmed or paralysed by them? How do we see clearly, through the forest of words and flashing of images, to what's really going on without first being blinded and then jaded?

We don't want to become the kind of nation described in Deuteronomy, 'A nation without sense, where there is no discernment.' If there's a quality that consumers, deliverers and makers of news need, it's the gift of discernment: the sound judgement that makes it possible to tell good from bad, recognize truth and integrity; and that makes for good governance. It can help us in the way we respond to news – the time we take to consider it, what to say about it, and see what is important. We need to stay engaged in order to be what scripture encourages us to be: a people 'who understand the times they're living in' so that they can 'know best what to do and discern what the end will be.'

11.7.2016

—

Friend in a coma

Ten weeks ago, a good friend of mine was checking something on a roof when he fell 30 feet to the ground. He received a serious head injury and remains in hospital in what is called a minimally conscious state.

On Monday I went to visit him with two of his friends. It was the first time we'd been able to see him and we were apprehensive about what we'd find. Would we recognize our friend and would our friend recognize us? Just before going in his wife and daughters, conscious of our fears, told us that he looked a bit rough but was still recognizably the man we knew. He was not able to respond on command, but he had occasionally shown flickers of awareness.

We each greeted him, taking his strong hand, and looked in to his one open eye for that glimmer of recognition or response. The broken body lying there did not seem to belong to the tough, ex-army man we knew, but he was still our friend; and over the next hour we talked to him, sang to him, prayed for him, had a metaphorical pint with him. Every blink or intake of breath became a precious event, as eloquent as any words. We felt sure he knew we were there – and that he was loved.

While he lay there between consciousness and unconsciousness, we ourselves hovered in and out of hope and doubt. Our friend's condition asked hard questions of our deepest fears and highest hopes. Does he really know we're here? Where's God in this? Will he heal him? Why has this happened? Should we just obey the psalmist who said, 'Be still and know that I am God', or should we implore the God who raises people from the dead to wake our friend to full consciousness?

The accidental is a reality we must face in a contingent world. It's a special challenge to anyone claiming to believe there's meaning to be found, especially in the toughest trauma. My friend's wife – a woman of faith – was honest about her anger at what had happened, and at her husband for threatening to leave this world too soon. Yet she admitted that her raging had taken her to a deeper, more intimate experience with God. The accident had re-ordered their lives around the fundamental hope that He loves us in all situations.

Over the years my friend has, more often than not, dropped me a line if he's caught a 'Thought For The Day'. In his no-nonsense way he'd always tell me exactly what he thought. Being a pragmatic, unsentimental Scot, he'd balk at the idea of his being the subject of a whole 'Thought', but I've been told that there's a radio next to his bed and that he's listening now. So, I don't know if you can hear me, Will, but I'm saying it anyway: you are not alone and you are loved.

9.9.2016

—

Irreconcilable differences

Since Brad Pitt and Angelina Jolie announced that they are to separate because of 'irreconcilable differences' much has been made of what those differences might be and what makes them irreconcilable. The pawing over what is essentially a private and painful matter will of course be justified by the couple's great celebrity. Irreconcilable differences make for good copy.

As a tireless ambassador for the United Nations, Jolie would probably be the first to point out that far graver concerns demand our attention. Thousands have died fleeing a conflict in Syria: the tragic outcome of irreconcilable differences. On Monday, campaigners from the international rescue committee laid 2,500 life jackets on the lawns of Parliament Square to represent refugees who had drowned trying to escape the wars in Syria and other countries; 350 had been worn by children.

Meanwhile in New York, the principle reconcilers of the conflict had gathered at the United Nations to discuss the cessation of hostilities, only to find their best efforts thwarted by an alleged Russian attack on a humanitarian aid convey. The heated exchanges between America and Russia threatened to end the hard-won ceasefire. 'This is not a joke' an exasperated US secretary of state John Kerry said, staring down his Russian counterpart Sergei Lavrov. He added, 'A chance for peace hangs by a very thin thread.' When the peacemakers themselves cannot find agreement, what hope is there for peace?

The job of the peacemaker tends to be a thankless one, and rarely grabs the headlines. Indeed, it is still a kind of miracle that there are people willing to sit in a room for days and weeks – sometimes with enemies – trying to reconcile the irreconcilable. This is, arguably, the very essence of the Christian message. As the prophet Isaiah says, 'We have lips that have spoken lies, hands stained with blood, fingers with guilt, and it is hard to find anyone calling for justice with integrity.' Incredibly, God's response is not to count these things against us, but to meet them head on and cancel them through His intervention in Christ, because to Him there are no differences that are irreconcilable.

In the face of bleak reports from Syria this morning, something of this divine ethic is needed more than ever to help keep the dialogue alive. The Apostle Paul spoke of those who do the work of reconciliation as Christ's ambassadors. Whether they profess faith or not, anyone trying to restore broken relationships between people and nations is an ambassador, for every act of reconciliation is in itself an echo of a divine act.

23.9.2016

—

Do you have a room for me?

The film *Cathy Come Home* was broadcast on BBC1 50 years ago. Directed by Ken Loach, it told the story of a young woman's descent into poverty and homelessness and was so realistic many of its 12 million viewers thought they were watching a documentary. The film was called 'The most successful piece of socially reforming drama on TV.' It was discussed in parliament, and the BBC switchboard was jammed by people wanting to give money. The charity Crisis was formed as a direct consequence of the drama. For years the actress who played Cathy was stopped by people in the street trying to press money into her hands.

Fifty years on and Ken Loach has made another film called *I Daniel Blake*, about a disabled man's struggle with the benefit system. While it's won the Palme D'Or at Cannes and garnered great critical praise, Loach himself doubts the film will have the same impact. Indeed, he wonders whether a *Cathy Come Home* would even get made now, let alone cause the outrage it did. Partly because viewers, he said, 'Would rather wallow in fake nostalgia,' but also because he thinks society has become more indifferent. Quoting scripture, this avowed atheist, says, 'We have lost the sense that we are our brothers' and sisters' keeper.'

Even people of different political persuasions agree that many of the problems raised in that film have not gone away. Tonight there will be around 3,500 people sleeping on the street. There are currently 75,000 households living in temporary accommodation. Meanwhile, the amount of social housing built every year has dropped dramatically since 1966.

Could it be that our idea of what a home is has changed? That it's less a basic human right and more something we earn the right to? An asset we manage as well as a place in which we live? Many factors contribute to homelessness, but the expense of property is certainly one of them. I'm relatively well-off, and I'm starting to worry about how my children are going to get on the property ladder; but what about the children whose parents aren't even on it?

In the film, when Cathy learns from social services that she has no home she is humiliated by their indifference. 'Why are you laughing?' she cries. 'Do you have a spare room in your house I could use?' In scripture indifference to poverty is seen as worse than contempt and the prophet's tongue is as unforgiving as a director's lens in pointing to its consequences.

When Jesus speaks of God's eternal accommodation, he is encouraging people to provide for the basic needs of others. If we are to avoid becoming indifferent, we need to make room for this issue, if not in our houses, then in our imaginations. It is storytellers like Loach who can do what the statistics can't – put us in the place of people who don't have what most of us do.

20.10.2016

—

A year of bad news

Back in January I met a friend in the street who was in tears having just heard the news that David Bowie had died. She was genuinely distraught. 'He was a part of my life,' she said. Before adding that it was 'Such a terrible way to start the year.'

If years were assessed in terms of artistic losses – particularly musicians – then 2016 has been an *Annus horribilis*, starting with Bowie and ending with George Michael, taking in the death of luminaries Prince, Leonard Cohen and many others. If you were inclined you could construct a narrative which imagined a curse at work, one that was robbing us of those who have brought a little joy and solace to our lives.

The litany of musical obituary has begun to feel like the unofficial soundtrack to a momentous year. There is no doubt that 2016 has given us seismic events, events that have led to social division that, some fear, will resonate well beyond it. With the merciless destruction of Aleppo, many are suggesting 2016 is the worst year they can remember.

Yet the most rudimentary grasp of history shows that 2016 wouldn't even make it into a top ten of worst years. If you were a British soldier obeying orders in 1916, or someone trying to survive the plague in 1347, or a mother fleeing Herod's massacre of the innocents 2,000 years ago, you'd have said the same thing.

People have always catastrophized the events of their day, and narratives of gloom have a particular momentum that is hard to resist. What is new is the means by which we absorb, discuss and react to news. Social media not only amplifies, it echoes and reinforces the narratives we want to hear, often to the exclusion of others. It encourages us to become our own historians, inclined to examine the world from our own perspective.

Of course, what is horrible or wonderful in any given year probably depends more on your personal experiences than world events, the micro more than the macro. If you were, say, a just-married, Leicester City supporting, cancer recovering, first time parent then you'd probably have a different perspective on 2016. It might have been your *Annus mirabilis*.

It says in Proverbs, 'Good news is like cold water to the thirsty.' Perhaps reactions to events this year show how thirsty we are. With perspective we might yet see the year 2016 less as an exception than as a slightly amplified version of the Same Old Story: the story of our struggle with ourselves and each other, with addiction or selfishness, sickness and death; the Same Old Story that is also woven with acts of courage and generosity, love and sacrifice, kindness and hope. As we pick through the rubble of what has been lost this year, let's look for the signs of life that will get us through the next.

28.12.2016

—

Fitter, happier, more productive

My friend has a smart watch that displays his pulse rate, how many steps he's taken that day, and hours he's slept. It's all about maximizing his fitness. As he shows it to me, he starts saying how, during a very stressful meeting, his heart rate tripled. Even as he is recalling this story his pulse rate starts rising; I wonder if the app is a help or a hindrance to his goal of achieving physical perfection.

At the start of the year, many of us experience an inner battle, between the self that has over-indulged and feels dissatisfied, and the self that wants to be, as Radiohead's song puts it, 'Fitter, happier, more productive, not drinking too much, taking regular exercise.' By now, many of us have instigated self-help strategies to achieve that lower pulse, deeper sleep and greater fruitfulness. Or, what some call 'self-optimizing'.

Authors Andre Spicer and Carl Cederstrom have explored this desire to be 'The best me I can be,' as well as the pressures that self-improvement puts on people. They suggest that the punishing ideals of this culture are unhelpful, even detrimental to our wellbeing. Their own experiment of trying to improve a particular area of their life each month ends with them discovering what we all know: that saying is easier than doing.

Yet this desire to be a better version of ourselves is more than faddish; it's fundamental and it raises important questions: What is the best I can be? Can I do it on my own? My annual attempt at self-optimizing usually involves negotiations around bread, beer, watching sport, taking exercise and a resolve to feed the soul. The latter is always the one I find hardest. I have a Bible designed to be read in a year and every year, to quote one of its proverbs, I return to my same old ways, 'like a dog returning to its vomit' and fail to get past January.

Curiously, it's this failure that can lead back to the source of the perfection being sought. The Benjamin Franklin quote that, 'God helps those who help themselves', often mistakenly attributed to the Bible, is really the opposite of what scripture is saying.

Scripture has much to say on self-help and its pitfalls. It may point to a perfection – to holiness. Achieving it doesn't depend on helping myself but on asking for God's help. When I fail it encourages me that 'The Lord is my helper;' and rather than seeking my own improvement it teaches me 'to lay aside my old self' in order to be renewed in mind, body and soul.'

Trying to be the best version of ourselves is a worthy aim, but it involves more than achieving a low pulse rate and higher productivity. It requires a trust that people find their best selves when they give up the self-help and look, instead, to the source of the perfection they desire.

4.1.2017

—

Aren't you still my enemy?

Growing up in 1970s Britain, the IRA were as much a part of the cultural noise as power cuts or the Bay City Rollers. The name was always in the news, and the news was always bad. My stepfather was in the British Army at that time and did several tours of duty in Northern Ireland at the height of the violence. For my family, news reports had added tension and the IRA was a name I came to fear and loath. I was 14 when the IRA killed Lord Mountbatten, and 18 soldiers at Warrenpoint the next day. The violence seemed to have this unstoppable momentum. I remember complaining, will there ever be a day when the news doesn't contain those three letters or the penetrating sound of an angry Northern Irish accent?

Forty years on and the death of Martin McGuinness – a former Provisional IRA chief of staff and initiator of the 'cutting edge' violence responsible for these deaths – gives a striking and unexpected answer to that question. For, as his obituary tells us, McGuinness dies not as the terrorist I thought he always would be, but as a former deputy minister of Northern Ireland. A man who was key to brokering the Good Friday Agreement and helping bring a peace that, back in the 1970s and 1980s, seemed about as likely as McGuinness shaking hands with Mountbatten's niece, The Queen.

For whether we like it or loath it, McGuinness' life-story maps a journey from violence to peace and demonstrates a transformation that is as heartening as it is difficult for some to take. For those directly affected by the violence he once condoned, perhaps he can never be forgiven. I think that we all struggle with the idea that someone can change, especially when that someone is an enemy; what happens to us when our enemies stop behaving as enemies and change their ways? Does it mean we have to change too? Is that just? Even though we may prefer reconciliation to strife, it's hard to let go when our identity is bound up in conflict.

Whatever we think of the man, McGuiness's journey echoes a gospel truth that a ministry of reconciliation is impossible if it's conditional upon our crimes forever being held against us. After all, we only make peace with our enemies. When I asked my stepfather how he felt about the news of McGuiness's death, he said his abiding image of him was the photograph of McGuinness laughing with his once bitter enemy, Ian Paisley. 'I still can't believe that actually happened,' he said. 'And it's unbelievable to me, even now.'

Thank God we live in a world where such unbelievable things are still possible.

22.3.2017

—

The story-telling creature

I have recently had four storylines running simultaneously in my head. There is one involving a dystopian future in which women are only permitted contact with men in order to conceive children, then there's a scenario where a black man is attacked by his own white girlfriend's family, another where someone's been murdered at a school fundraiser in Monterrey, and one where the anti-corruption police have just discovered the truth about the death of a forensic officer.

There was a point during the Bank Holiday – while devouring novel, TV box-set, play and film – where I wondered if my appetite for stories had got out of control. Yet it seems I'm not alone in my hunger. Seven and a half million people watched the series finale of *Line of Duty* on Sunday. Television drama is enjoying a new golden age. Last year over £4 billion-worth of books were sold in the UK; and stories are being shared and consumed every minute through social media, blogs and news. While formats come and go, stories old and new are here to stay. At least until the end of time and maybe after that.

Humans are the story-telling creatures. Not one society, even when prohibited, has ever stopped telling them. They are as inevitable as gravity and almost as necessary to our existence as food. Even at night, when the body goes to sleep, the mind stays awake telling itself tales.

This appetite must reside, in part, in our story-shaped existence: we love narrative because our lives are narratives. People are stories – her-stories and his-stories. As the Roman poet Horace observed: change the names in a tale for your own and you become its subject. Our lives may not seem as neatly plotted as a box set, as clever and lyrical as a novel, or as beautifully lit as a movie, but in the best of them we recognize something of ourselves; they invite us to enter in and take us with them. They allow us to be a part of the story.

In this sense, faith and narrative share the same page. My own faith is less about accepting a set of maxims and rules than about believing a story. The gospel narrative is a story before it's a creed – and even the creed is a story. It's one about a particular God in a particular time and place, who enters into this concrete but temporal life in all its messy contingency. I'd even go as far to say that story is *the* form in and through which this particular God chooses to speak to people. As the words become flesh, mundanity and transcendence mix and we are taken from the mud to the manger, from the dust to the stars. From the beginning to the end.

3.5.2017

—

A tale of two towers

On a clear day I can see some of London's landmarks from the top of the house. The arches of Wembley Stadium to the north, the BT Tower in the centre and, dominating the eastern skyline, the Shard which is five years old this week. Sadly, London has another landmark now, one that draws the eye and stops the heart. The burned-out shell of Grenfell Tower – a building clad in sackcloth and ashes, standing as an admonishment to other, grander buildings. What used to be a panoramic view is now a sort of morality tale. A Tale of Two Towers.

Grenfell and the Shard are not that far apart, a few miles as the helicopter flies, but they represent polarized experiences of life in this city. For some, one is now a tragic symbol of neglect, incompetence and under-investment; the other a shiny, hubristic symbol of excess. Yet despite inhabiting different universes, these two towers share the same ground. Their fates are connected and you don't need to be a poet or a preacher to see the connections.

As the displaced people of Grenfell wait for new, permanent accommodation from which to rebuild their lives; news comes that the ten penthouses at the top of the Shard (with a reported collective value of £200 million) apparently remain unsold and, according to the building's management company, 'empty shells.' Shocking though this sounds, the Shard is not an anomaly. London is full of empty luxury flats in shiny glass towers that people can't afford; investments for some, but homes to few.

Whenever there is a tragedy involving human error, it is usual for someone to say that 'lessons must be learned.' What can we learn from this? Learning lessons has to be about more than receiving information or facts; it requires some genuine change of mind, heart and then action. Of course, the Grenfell fire is more than a lesson to be learned, it's a lived disaster that awaits a deeper explanation. The Shard's difficulties are more than just symbolic of excessive wealth, but there is a line than connects these two towers.

In Luke's Gospel, Jesus tells a mini parable, short enough to quote here in full, that offers some insight into what that connection might be: 'Suppose one of you wants to build a tower. Will he not first sit down and estimate the cost to see if he has enough money to complete it? For if he lays the foundation and is not able to finish it, everyone who sees it will ridicule him, saying, "This person began to build and was not able to finish".

If I could extract from this short tale a lesson that speaks to these situations, one that might change things, it would be, 'Let's stop building towers that are too expensive to buy, or too dangerous to live in, and instead estimate the true value of building homes in which people can live.

6.7.2017

—

Dark is the new black

'What do I watch next?' my friend asked. *Game of Thrones* was over and he'd finished series one of *Ozark*. I said there was a new show about a serial-killer that's told backwards; there was a psychosexual whodunnit on ITV and if that was no good he could watch the drama about a cop who takes revenge when his son is murdered. Later, I wondered if this is how we measure out our lives now: watching box sets of ever-increasing darkness.

I confess I watch a lot of this stuff, and that I once wrote scripts for *Silent Witness*, a show always built around a dead body. There's certainly an appetite for these things. Look at the amount of crime drama being made. Death and violence sell, and makers of today's dramas know it. Recently I was pitching ideas to a TV company when a producer said, with great portent, 'What we're looking for is something dark.' I had to stop myself from saying, 'Isn't everyone?'

It seems that television drama is now in a kind of arms race, with each series trying to be bleaker and blacker than the last, with ever increasing body counts and more extreme ways of killing people. While the better shows portray the violence as necessary, it often just seems gratuitous. It's as though the makers fear they won't hold our attention unless they shock us every five minutes. Increasingly I watch these shows using the fast forward button to get through the gore. Dark is the new black.

Except, of course, it isn't new. Dorothy Sayers once wrote, 'Death provides the mind with a greater fund of innocent enjoyment than any single subject,' and it was ever thus. The trouble is that if things get too dark no one can see anything. Most art forms need the chiaroscuro, the light and the shade, to connect. Real life – for all its suffering and trauma – is never one note and the creators of the best shows recognize this. There has to be humour and humanity, some illumination, to see through all this dark.

What explains the fascination? Is it, as John's Gospel puts it, that 'People loved darkness rather than the light?' Or is it something else? While some watch for the violence, I think most watch hoping for an interesting plot, for justice to be done, and for the truth to be exposed. There's a need for conclusion in a narrative and moral sense. Most dramas – no matter how pretentiously noir – are looking for this resolution, this redemption, and are relying on our innate desire for it.

The most powerful stories may need darkness, but they also need light to be believable. This is as true of the gospels as it is of *Game of*

Thrones. The gospel drama is bad news before it's good, and a lot of violence, suffering and death has to be faced before the light breaks in.

15.9.2017

—

Bad theology kills

It's a week for speeches – President Trump's maiden address to the UN, Aung San Suu Kyi's on the Rohinga crisis, Prime Minister May's to the EU in Florence today. It remains to be seen whose words – or choice phrase – will be remembered, or which speech will have a lasting impact on the world.

There's certainly plenty to remember from Donald Trump's. His threat to totally destroy North Korea, the ridiculing of its leader as 'Rocket Man' and his insulting of Iran stick in the mind; but among the bluster the most disturbing element for me was his division of the world into 'the righteous many' and 'the wicked few'. We've heard this kind of rhetoric before, and indeed, from a previous US president. It draws on a belief that life is a struggle between the forces of good and evil. It is often described as Manichean, and I do think it brings dangers with it.

Manicheism was actually a dualistic religious philosophy taught by the Iranian prophet Mani in the third century. It was rejected by orthodox Christianity as a heresy and later by Islam, yet it often surfaces in the fundamentalist extremes of these faiths and can be used by those wanting to stir up a binary nationalist feeling by calling 'them' the bad people and 'us' the good. In my view, it's not only bad theology (which, as we keep seeing, can kill), but it's not what the gospel or the general weight of scripture tells us about God, ourselves or the world. Whole people groups can't be righteous any more than whole countries can be evil. The prophets constantly warned against thinking in these terms. Righteousness was not a birth-right.

It's a tricky word, righteousness, marrying the concept of goodness to an idea of justification. It has something to do with right action – seeking justice for the poor and the outcast, as well as speaking with respect – but it has nothing to do with where we come from. Plus, it is something we should be very careful to claim for ourselves – and deny others.

Jesus tells a parable about a religious leader and a tax-collector who went to a temple to pray. The former prayed about himself, thanking God that he was not like those other 'bad' people, and pointing to his good deeds; but the tax collector, feeling unworthy, simply asked for God's forgiveness. No prizes for guessing which one walked away justified before God. 'Everyone who exalts himself will be humbled; he who humbles himself will be exalted.'

In a world of wild rhetoric and hot boasts, we have to listen carefully to hear what's really being said. The words of the righteous have been described as being like 'a fountain of life' or even 'apples of gold.' Perhaps when anyone makes a speech claiming to be righteous, we should check for the evidence of that life and look for its fruit.

22.9.2017

—

God, make me famous

In 1976 a survey was conducted in the US asking young people to list their life goals. Fame came fifteenth out of 16 possibilities. By 2012, another poll suggested that being famous was the most popular life goal among a group of 10–12-year-olds. It wasn't about being famous for doing anything in particular, just a desire to be known, preferably by as many people as possible.

It could well be that we are living in a golden age of narcissism. An era where self-regard is at a zenith (or nadir) and the desire to be someone, to be famous, has become the defining characteristic of its people – from kids through to the leaders of nations. It's a desire neatly parodied by the band Arcade Fire in their lyric 'God, make me famous and, if you can't, just make it painless.'

While leaders should know better, those ten-year-olds can hardly be blamed. They are assaulted by the pulse beat and images of self-regard on a daily basis – and at a pace that is quickening every year. All reinforced by a culture which tells them – in schools, movies and media – you are special, don't put limits on yourself. 'Become a better you.'

Positive statements that in the wrong hands quickly sound like a gospel of self-trust, a confidence-trick that creates unsustainable anxiety, painful comparison and future disappointment. Dangerous because it affects people just when they are most acutely conscious of their developing selves. In a scene from a new film called *Lady Bird*, a mother defends nagging her 18-year-old daughter by saying, 'I want you to be the very best version of yourself that you can be.' To which her daughter replies, 'What if this is the best version of me?'

Fame seems to offer a quick way to get approval, to take a short cut to that 'better me', while avoiding the baleful business of dealing with our deeper fears, one of which may well be a fear of not being known. If there is a better version of ourselves to be found, where do we find it? Certainly not on our own. We need the redemptive assistance of others. It can come with different faces; it *might* be that nagging parent; the stern teacher, that miss-no-trick, iron-sharpens-iron friend – or in another way, a God who points to a different definition of self.

Christ, in his Sermon on the Mount, offers what might be considered a total inversion of how to be famous when he describes the characteristics of those who have found themselves. The beatitudes are a quiet, unflashy and unexciting list but, swap the word famous for blessed and you get the point: famous are the compassionate, the overlooked, the humble. They may not shout as loudly as fame's claims, but they recognize that we are much more than approval-seeking machines and suggest what it might look like to be being truly known.

27.10.2017

—

Finding lost boys

Near Mosul in Iraq there is a camp that holds around 1,500 women and children, the families of former ISIS fighters. Known as 'The Daeshis' by the locals, they are, among outcasts, perhaps the most reviled in the world.

My friend is a doctor who has just returned from Iraq where she worked in the trauma hospital treating the injured and sick from both sides of the war. While she had conflicting emotions in helping people responsible for horrendous atrocities her colleagues, the Iraqi medical staff, had to go the extra mile to help the relatives of people who had killed their own kith and kin.

To make things worse, many of the ISIS women and children refused to be treated, touched or helped in any way by the medical staff, particularly the Iraqi Christians. Some of the women stared silently, hands balled into fists. Some children cried in reaction to being shown kindness – as though kindness was a perversion.

What to do with these children of ISIS? The hospital had little in the way of rehabilitation facilities, but a TV screen was set up to show DVDs. My friend said it had a remarkable effect on some. One of the most resistant children sat in front of *Finding Nemo* transfixed for two hours, a look of wonder on his face. It might just have been the colour and sound, television had been forbidden under the regime, but this film was in a language he didn't understand and something was getting through. What was he seeing? Was this tale about a lost fish who is trying to find its parents resonating? Was it the shock of discovering that there were other ways of seeing the world; that there were other stories out there?

War is a voracious thief robbing children of their childhood. No child can be blamed for the crimes of their parents; or should be punished for being caught up in yet another war waged by adults. The children of ISIS, like the lost boys of Sudan or the child soldiers of Uganda, are coerced into fighting that war. They were told a terrible story; they have, to quote Jesus, been given a snake instead of a fish. The poison of that snake paralyses the mind – and crushes the soul. To do this to children, he said, is a spiritual crime exacting a very tough justice.

An innocent robbed of their innocence is still innocent, still in need of our help, still in need of rehabilitation. Skin can be stitched and blood can be replenished, but the trauma and wounds to the psyche, especially of these children, needs a deeper and profounder repairing. Disney isn't enough, but as this lost boy shows, it's a start; there are better stories for our children out there and telling them is key to their future healing.

30.11.2017

—

The archbishop's pause

A few years ago on this radio programme, John Humphrys was interviewing the then Archbishop of Canterbury, Rowan Williams. It was the day after the Beslan massacre and the presenter asked the minister the difficult question: Where was God when those children were being killed? Williams requested permission to take a moment before answering. What followed was either an awkward hesitation or a brave and necessary pause. There was complete radio silence for eight, nine, maybe ten seconds – a long time on live radio, an eternity on a programme that relies on rapid reaction. The sound of a person thinking about what they should say before saying it created a crackling tension in the studio; while Humphrys waited respectfully for the archbishop, you could feel the producers urging him to say something lest listeners think the station had gone off air.

I can't fully recall the words Rowan Williams used after that pause, but I remember the silence. I think the archbishop knew that even the cleverest response would fail to explain such a raw and painful event and that this most difficult of theological questions was impossible to answer to everyone's satisfaction. In resisting the temptation to say something immediately for the sake of filling the air waves, he was willing to risk sounding as though he had no answer at all. Yet in a way, his silence was part of the answer, an acknowledgement that some questions can't be answered with words.

That pause 14 years ago can still give us pause today at a time when it feels as if the culture is growing increasingly intolerant of the considered response. There is an ever-quickening demand for speedy reaction, instant opinion, ready certainties – and we have the technology to facilitate this urge. This is an age that values reflexes over reflection. Where a soundbite is better than a sound chewed. Giving a bad answer is better than giving no answer and saying nothing is a kind of weakness. Reflecting is for holy men and mirrors.

This addiction to reacting is, I'd suggest, a tyranny that's corrupting both private and public discourse. It's in danger of making us impatient with the things that really do require careful rumination, time and thought: the painstaking brokering of a peace deal, the reading of a book, the education of a child – all the complex areas of human activity that shun the fast answer.

Fools will continue to rush in to fill the silence – especially when their identity is built on having to say something and say it quickly, loudly and first. Yet silence is golden when it protects us from saying something needless or glib. On the day of Christ's death, the mob taunted him with a question: 'Where is your God now?' Christ gave no comment, not because he didn't have anything to say, but because I think he knew that his silence was part of the answer.

28.12.2017

—

Adulthood

It is an awesome privilege to have a child and an unexpected grace to see that child become an adult. My daughter has just turned 18 and has technically made the transition to adulthood. This week we symbolically said good night to the girl and good morning to the woman. I say symbolically because the definition of adulthood – when it starts, what it is – can't really be nailed to a particular age, and it evades easy definition. Is it just about getting the vote? There is a proposal to extend the franchise in Wales to 16-year-olds, but would this make them adults? The new adult in our house can now vote, but she's living at home, economically dependent and still growing up.

Adulthood has been defined as the age at which a person attains a stable independent role in society; but what if that is delayed or cancelled altogether by circumstance? According to Brilliant Maps, someone living in Europe doesn't gain financial independence until they are nearly 30. While many young in the West remain infantilized by economics, children in other parts of the world grow up too soon because of war or become adults more quickly because their way of life runs to a different rhythm.

What exactly does it mean to be an adult? We interact with them every day and often see them, some in positions of great responsibility, displaying less than adult behaviour. At the same time, we see that children are capable of blindingly mature insight and possessed of a wisdom beyond their years. Why else would Christ refer to them as being natural inheritors of His kingdom? Of course, the world wouldn't function if it were only populated by Peter Pans; but there are qualities children possess that adults need to retain.

When my youngest turned 18, someone pointed out that there were no longer any children in the house. To which I replied, 'Unless you count me.' This wasn't said completely in jest. I once heard an old preacher say he hoped he grew up before he grew old. It was an acknowledgement that the process of maturity, what the Apostle Paul calls 'growing in stature and wisdom', is ongoing and that, this side of the grave, may never be accomplished.

I think this reality is liberation for any parent feeling they have somehow failed if they haven't delivered a fully a formed adult by the time they turn 18. Yes, we need to help them move on from 'drinking milk' to 'eating meat' as scripture puts it, and to 'leave behind childish ways', but some of us never fully grow up, even when we're parents. If becoming an adult can be marked once, on a particular day, growing to maturity starts the day we are born and doesn't stop until the day we die.

2.2.2018

—

Gimme shelter

There are many mansions in this kingdom; but not everyone gets to sleep in one. Today there are officially just under 5,000 people sleeping rough in the UK (although the charity Crisis puts the figure at 9,000). There may be a shortage of easy remedies, but there's no shortage of good will. This winter, many people have pitched up in town halls, chapels or school buildings to help serve meals and provide temporary accommodation for the homeless.

Every Wednesday volunteers from my neighbourhood gather at a church and convert it into a hostel for the night. We cook, lay the tables, serve the guests and then join them for the meal. Initially, it's an awkward communion of the sheltered and the unsheltered. The question you want to ask is how did you end up here? The charity advises against getting personally involved, but some guests are happy to tell their stories. It soon becomes clear that homelessness is an umbrella term for a number of social concerns. It might be triggered by a family tragedy or a mental health issue; by bad luck or bad choices. There is no one route to this situation.

For a while, the differences between us and the guests are obscured by the fact that we are all under one roof, eating the same food, discussing the same things. The more we share, the greater there is a sense among the volunteers that given different circumstances 'It could be one of us out there, looking for a bed for the night.'

Later, over the washing up, some judgement started to creep in, when someone suggested that a particular guest had clearly brought their situation upon themselves, while another guest had blamed everyone else for their plight. We agreed that homelessness was complicated, but the moment we started debating the reasons for it, something was lost. The person became a problem, that fragile communion was broken. We needed to remind ourselves that we were not there to attribute blame or be counsellors, but to feed people and see that they had a bed for the night. For as James puts it, 'What use is it if your brother or sister doesn't have enough food for the day and you say "good luck, eat well, stay warm" but do nothing to meet their bodily needs?'

Jesus avoided being drawn into arguments about cause and effect and discouraged his followers from speculating about people's problems – as He knew it would lead to judgement. Instead he identified himself with the homeless to such an extent that scripture goes as far as suggesting that if we take up their cause we may find

Him. No one has seen God, says the gospel writer, but you might find him among the destitute and dejected.

Walking back to my shelter that night, I couldn't help thinking that if such a God existed, He would still be out there, looking for the ones who have nowhere to go.

8.2.2018

—

Clinging to power

When a country's leader refuses to step down, they are often described as 'clinging to power' as though power were a physical thing than can be grasped, a solid object that can be held and possessed. Last night it was South African leader Jacob Zuma, who finally relinquished his grip. Last year it was Robert Mugabe; who can say which leader's fingers will be prized from power next.

The dangers of power seem to increase for those who have more of it. History offers a long list of leaders who have found it hard to give it up without tenaciously, sometimes brutally, trying to hold on to it, like a child refusing to share a prized toy. Status has something to do with it, and the money (as is allegedly the case with Zuma). Having control over people and a sometimes unchecked ability to have your way can't help. Add to this the belief that you can do the job better than anyone else, and that your identity in inseparable from your role, then no wonder leaders find it hard to give it up.

Power's corrupting effect is something even the most transparent democratic systems can't fully guard against, but I think it still comes down to the character of the individual in question. Which is why we need to be good at spotting those most likely to become addicted to 'a worldly crown,' or seek power for its own sake. It seems that the more a leader tries to get hold of power, the more likely it is to get hold of them. Conversely, those who hold it lightly are the ones best able to handle it more responsibly, and less likely to hang on, and remain, as Milton puts it, 'A spectacle of ruin and scorn.'

The footage of Obama leaving the Whitehouse demonstrated this well. It showed a man who, one day, had more worldly power than anyone, walking away without it the next. As he departed through the colonnades of power someone asked if he was going to miss it. 'Of course,' he said; but later when asked how he felt about giving it up he said, 'Just fine'. It wasn't his to keep.

I think a leader (of any kind) who recognizes how fragile their power is and where it comes from is more likely to use it well, in the service of others. It takes a certain confidence not to have to be in control or to rule all the time. An acetic discipline of the ego is crucial for allowing an institution to carry on when you are no longer there.

In Milton's *Paradise Regained*, Satan asks Jesus why he won't take up the worldly power that's on offer. Jesus answers, 'He who reigns over his passions, desires and fears is more of a King.' It's a reminder that the most important power struggle of all takes place within the character of the individual.

15.2.2018

—

Faith in imagination

Every summer, literary pilgrims gather in a field in Wales to celebrate writers and their works. With its valley of tents, the Hay Festival looks like a well-attended revivalist meeting, except here the faithful are drawn not by *The* Word, but by a belief in the power of words.

Once upon a time literature and faith more readily shared the same tent. Questions of doubt and belief found a natural place in novels such as *Brothers Karamazov, The Outsider* and *The Power and*

The Glory. For writers there was no fear of, or literary embarrassment in, addressing what are sometimes called the First Order questions: Does life have meaning? Is evil an entity? Is there life after death? Is there a God?

Then culture reached a rough consensus that these questions had been settled (by science, psychology and philosophy) and that the answer to all of them was 'no.' Faith as a subject for literature was pushed to the margins of the page. Redemption, if it existed, was something a person had to find for themselves, without the help of outside agency. The miraculous was not to be trusted. This life may be a wonder, but it is random and finite and there is no God to thank for it.

The experience of faith is still an everyday reality for millions of people, a vital part of the drama of their lives. It's rarely re-imagined as a creative, attractive or subtle thing. When it is depicted in stories it's often extreme: the overbearing religious parent, the abusive spiritual leader, the dystopian theocracy. Perhaps the nature of belief – the inner workings of the soul, the encounter with the transcendent – eludes easy capture on the page. Or maybe we just need new ways of imagining these things.

The strapline for Hay this year is, 'Imagine the world', and it's an important idea for imagination in a space where professor, poet and priest can all pitch their tents. A scientist needs imagination to envisage unseen outcomes, a reader relies on it to believe in the world of a novel and it's essential to exercise imagination when trying to understand the divine. Faith, like literature, can't survive without metaphor, symbol or story. Faith without imagination becomes dry, legalistic and humourless. It's why fundamentalism (of the believing or unbelieving kind) fears it; it's easier to follow rules and believe in measurable certainties than in life's ambiguities and possibilities.

Imagination is one of humanity's great gifts. It allows us to perceive that reality is not just about what can be seen or quantified. Writers instinctively know this and rely on it because there really are 'more things in heaven and earth, than are dreamt of in our philosophy.' A novel requires and tries to justify the assent of its readers, asking them to believe in its world. Writers need readers to be believers, and when this happens a small miracle occurs.

2.6.2018

—

To worry or not to worry

Let us spare a thought for the thousands of students sitting exams today. While writing this, my own daughter was sitting an A level English paper on *Hamlet*, and probably trying to spell quintessence as well remember what it means.

Upon the eve of the exam, I joked with her that were Hamlet to sit the A level he'd never have got going. His will would have been stuck in neutral. Paralysed by both the choice of what to say and the seeming pointlessness of it all. Of course, my own antic disposition was all part of a parental strategy, employed to ease her nerves, to make light of it, to help reduce the stress levels which, if reports are to be believed, are at all time high among our students, from GCSE through to degree level.

Exams have always been an unpleasant if necessary reality. They still supply the plotline of my one recurring nightmare in which I'm either late for the exam or haven't read the books – or both. Yet the epidemic of anxiety being experienced by today's generation seems new, and a confluence of factors – future debts, uncertain job prospects and a relentless competitive comparison – are all contributing.

It's silly to pretend that exam results don't have consequences. A grade either way can determine a destination, the people you meet, the job you get, but something's gone badly awry in the collective perspective when students feel their very life hangs on a percentage point.

While the symptoms of worry may be more profound now, I think the source is the same as it's always been. Part of it is, as Shakespeare puts it, that, 'We know what we are but not what we may be.' This fear of a future we cannot control is not exclusive to students; it is the human condition.

'To worry or not to worry. That is the question.' It's this question that Jesus addresses in his famous if sometimes maligned speech, in which he says, 'Do not worry about tomorrow,' while pointing to the lilies of the field and birds of the air, sustained by God's care and therefore carefree. These sound like pat words to offer someone who is anxious. Unless it's possible that this same care covers our exam results, our future careers and our lives. Then these words can be heard as a wisdom vital for living; calling us to keep a right perspective rather let it be bent out of shape by anxiety. These words are a counter to the lie that says if you fail, you are worthless.

As parents and as a society, we have to work hard to keep this balance. When I tell my daughter that it doesn't matter if she doesn't make the grade, I absolutely mean it; not because I don't think making the grade matters, but because, for me, she already has. That, I think, is the gospel truth.

8.6.2018

—

Virtue signalling

A couple of years ago, the phrase Virtue Signalling started appearing in articles and posts and soon achieved ubiquity. It is roughly defined as someone expressing an opinion that is designed to garner approval from people and make them look morally superior. The virtue signaller doesn't necessarily have to do anything about the issue. They just have to let everyone know they are thinking about it.

Their opinion can even be disguised in the form of a negative, such as 'I hate 4 by 4s' (which really means, 'Like all good people, I am environmentally conscious').

It's a clever term and its appeal is easy to grasp. For as well as being pithy, it has the whiff of truth. It's a modern way of calling out people who parade their views and actions to look good or, in old money, someone who is holier than thou. A quick glance at social media shows how appealing the phrase is and how often it is bandied about. There are whole websites and channels dedicated to calling out the hypocrites. With perceived offenders mercilessly policed and exposed. There is no shortage of stones being thrown.

The trouble is, the phrase has become toxic. It's too often used as a lazy put-down that can lead to a scatter gun stoning of all kinds of people; it's become a weapon that stigmatizes responses that are sometimes genuine and potentially virtuous. Worse still, the phrase infects anyone who uses it with the very things they are calling out. To accuse someone of virtue signalling is to commit two sins for the price of one: you are essentially making a judgement – about someone's actions or inactions, while at the same time vainly puffing yourself up at their expense. The phrase makes hypocrites of us all.

Virtue signalling is really a new term for a very old practice, one that goes back to the cave and can be witnessed in any primary school playground or democratic parliament. It was categorically addressed by Jesus in his warning to beware of practicing our righteousness in front of people in order to win their approval. Don't make a great fanfare of your good deeds, he said; instead, if you can, give in secret because God sees your actions and your virtue does not go unnoticed.

Ultimately, a virtuous person shouldn't care whether their good deeds are seen or not. Years ago, in a period of my life when I was struggling to pay the rent, someone posted a thousand pounds in cash through my letter box. It came anonymously, without fanfare or even a note. I tried to find out who had given me the money, even asking a couple of worthy suspects, but I never found out who it was.

The invisible giver has stayed anonymous to this day. No hint of a signal has been offered but their virtue remains intact.

22.6.2018

—

A love supreme

This is a song
Without a melody
A call to tune in and celebrate
This thing called music
Which, in a world where few agree
And nothing sounds the same,
Still changes lives, as well as moods
In language not everyone can read
But everyone perceive.

It's both background noise
And vital hum
Humanity's constant giving thrum
It fits the occasion
Joyous celebration and quiet devotion,
It starts the revolution
Brings the revelation.
Via valleys deep it
Reaches depression
On mountains high
Transcends explanation.

It can't be proved
But is stronger than steel
Louder than bombs,

A love supreme

It hits but doesn't hurt.
There is no right or wrong
One man's dirge
Is another man's song.
There's no one way to say it
Some sing you can't stop it
That we're lost in it
That rivers clap their hands to it
Others that life's a mistake without it
That love is fed by it

It's the wine that fills the cup.
It makes the people come together
The bourgeois and the rebel
It knows no class or race,
Cuts across the politic
That no matter what state we're in
There'll still be music we can sing
We just need to stay in tune
Not break the harmony
Kill the melody, play the off key
Strike the wrong note.
Bad people love good music
Good people love the bad
That's not the point
Everyone has a tune
And the tune is key
Come as you are, Come and see
Come all ye faithful, Come on everybody
Listen to the music
Thank you for the music
Who can live with out it
God only knows what we'd do without it.

Godbothering

It gives soul to the universe
Wings to the mind
Evokes without words
Our greatest joys our deepest fears
Einstein thought in music
To sing his equations
Bach made agreeable harmony
To make his devotions
It's maths to the mathematician
Audible waves to the physician
We're all part of the composition.
It's everybody's business
You can sell it or you can buy it
But no-one owns it
It's free as a bird, it's all right, it does its thing

Music. It's divine
Let those who have ears, hear
A transcendence we can gain
A way to talk to angels
And sing God's praise.
It makes a way
To express the inexpressible,
A thing you can't see
More real than things you touch
More touching than a thing.
It's a tune we can all hear.

If you don't like the words
Truth, mercy, love
Are songs we can hymn
It's the same refrain
It's a Love Supreme

A wonderful thing.
We are the giver and the taker
We are the melody of the maker
So if we're the song
Then let's sing.

28.9.2018

—

Peacebuilding

Every year a group of lexographers decides which new words to add to the dictionary. They have to consider a couple of things: Is the word in widespread use? Does it have staying power or is it a passing fad? Recent words include hangry, newsjacking and Kompromat (you can look them up). If words reflect the preoccupations and values of a culture, I wonder what these words say about ours.

This year a group of people involved in peacebuilding have proposed that the word peacebuilding be given a dictionary definition. It seems reasonable, they argue, that the activities of the many people around the world who are committed to the prevention of conflict and the promotion of a lasting peace be included in the lexicon alongside warmongers, firebrands and rabble-rousers. As far back as 1992, the UN defined peacebuilding, alongside peacekeeping and peacemaking (both already in the dictionary), as a distinct and essential means to helping war-torn societies transition from violence to peace.

Peacebuilding is, by nature, an unheralded and hidden activity, and in an age of look-at-me showoffery (not a word yet), it isn't as exciting as warmongering or as sexy as cyber-hacking. It connotes something difficult. Something that requires stamina and patience. It is also fragile: it is far easier to knock down than build up, to monger or trade in violence than in peace. A city raised over millennia can be razed in a day – it takes years to nurture a life, seconds to end one.

Many of us can recall the atrocities of our age and name the perpetrators and their terrible deeds, but may struggle to name what the prophet Isaiah called repairers of the breach or fixers of broken walls. I can name some famous peacebuilders, but my list of destructive aggressors and the weapons they used far outguns them.

One famous peacebuilder, Martin Luther King, once said that 'The arc of the moral universe is long but it bends towards justice.' Some thinkers such as Stephen Pinker endorse that hopeful trajectory with statistics that suggest a less violent mankind is evolving. I want to believe they're right, but we're going to need a lot of peacebuilders to keep us on track.

We live in a time of great verbal as well as physical violence, and verbal aggression is often a precursor to the physical. Words matter. They are symbols and have the power to change things for good or ill. Someone once said, 'Blessed are the peacemakers.' I believe this, but the inheritors of peace are also blessed. We may not all feel it, but we are blessed in this country because we have inherited a peace built upon the efforts of others who tried to weave together the torn fabric of society and create something new.

It would be good to live in a country that acknowledged the word for that.

3.10.2018

—

Killing the messenger

Telling the truth is and has always been a dangerous activity. It can bring down the mighty, it leads to the toppling of palaces and kings, but it is especially perilous wherever there is contempt for freedom, and the powerful can kill the messenger with impunity.

The disappearance and possible murder of Saudi reporter Jamal Khashoggi in Turkey, and the rape and murder of Victoria Marinova in Bulgaria, this week highlight how dangerous this truth business is. Since 1990, 2,500 journalists have been killed while doing their work. While many of those died in combat situations, there seems to be a growing trend of investigative journalists being assassinated by governments who don't want their story told.

Khashoggi's plight feels emblematic of the direction the world is taking. A Saudi man leaves his country because of his outspoken criticism of its leader, seeks paperwork in a country that is itself reported to have detained 245 journalists, in order to return to another country whose own leader has described the media as the enemy of the people. This level of jeopardy seems like something from a movie. 'Get out your notebook,' says Bob Woodward's source in *All The President's Men*. 'There's more. A lot more. And your lives are in danger.' Tragically, for Khashoggi, it seems his work may have cost him his life (though the Saudi government strenuously deny this).

'He who allows oppression shares the crimes,' said Erasmus. In a small way these words apply to those of us who listen to and consume the news on programmes like this, programmes that rely on and can't survive without reporters who are prepared to look into and say the difficult thing about powerful people and dangerous regimes. If we say nothing and do nothing to defend them who can be relied on to tell us how things really are? There would surely be no news worth hearing.

A long-dead messenger called Amos once spoke truth to the government of his day. He delivered the news to the king and it was very bad indeed. He said, you're heading for destruction via fire and locust; but (and this was the good news) you can still change, if you reset things. Then Amos described a plumb-line – an instrument for measuring how straight and true a building is – and he challenged the king and his people to use it – to realign themselves before the palace toppled on their heads.

A prophet's job was not to predict the future but to call out the present. Like a good investigative journalist, they had to trust their source, describe what was going on, however ugly and corrupt it might be, whoever it might offend, even at the risk of being killed for saying it. They had to name names, even when prefixed by the title prince or president. It's a dangerous but vital job for it leaves those who hear the message with the chance to reset things and do what is right.

10.10.2018

—

'Snowflake' generation

Among the many crises that seem to be looming, there is one that nobody quite wants to own or knows how to solve. Partly because its causes are so complex, but also because its effects are still unfolding.

The rise in depression, anxiety and suicide among 16–24-year-olds – or, as some pejoratively call them, The Snowflake Generation – is beginning to look like an epidemic. Suicides have doubled in 20 years. Teenagers today are more likely to be depressed than those during The Great Depression and, according to psychologist Peter Gray, since the 1950s things have got better for the old but much worse for the young.

What's going on? In the panicked scramble to answer this question, some blame parents. Some blame teachers. This week, the chief of Ofsted warned that schools can't be substitute parents. Others (usually older people) blame the Snowflake Generation itself. The term snowflake comes from the book and film *Fight Club*, which features the line 'You are *not* special, you are *not* a beautiful and unique snowflake.' It's since become a putdown for a generation that's seen as over-sensitive and supposedly lacking in resilience.

What generation in history has had to grow up through a technological revolution that, for all its wonders, has brought so many unforeseen deleterious effects: all-day distraction, a fragmentation of concentration, insidious amplified comparison, a relentless 24-hour fight for attention? Answer? None. This generation is an unwitting guinea pig for something unprecedented. They may not have fought in wars, but I'd say they are in a battle. A largely hidden fight involving the self, the mind, the emotions. To blame them for a mental fragility is to do two things: to ignore the problem and to deny our part in it. As Jeremiah puts it, 'The fathers have eaten sour grapes and the children's teeth are set on edge.'

In their song 'I'm Scum,' The English punk band Idles make a virtue of this supposed over-sensitivity, defiantly yelling the warning that 'This snowflake's an avalanche,' suggesting that this generation may be more resilient than we think, but they'll bury us all unless we face the problem.

Curiously, sensitivity is probably the key. Responses to this fragility need to be tender as well as urgent; creative as well as practical. Thankfully, there are people (of all ages) who are improvising hopeful responses, trying to find ways to restore mental health among the young. Solutions that include play therapy, dance, mindfulness, technological de-tox, as well programmes like the Healthy Mind Project that help students develop emotional resilience and self-efficacy.

A prophet once described a world where parents turned their hearts to their children and children their hearts to their parents. Perhaps it's time to do away with generational demarcation lines. Millennials, Baby Boomers, Generation X. We all need the same things: we all yearn for a sense of worth and health. To be, like snowflakes, special, beautiful and unique.

3.12.2018

—

Prediction versus prophecy

It's the time of year for making predictions and if even half of what's foretold comes to pass, 2019 is apparently shaping up to be a good year for the Cassandras. They're saying it's going to be a bad year, and not just because it ends with a nine.

Happily, people are notoriously poor at predicting the future. Scientists have shown that we have a tendency to construct predictions from our wishes or terrors rather than actual data; and, even then, the super-forecasters who are paid to get things right can get it badly wrong. Like the banker who told Henry Ford the horse was here to stay, or Michael Fish the weatherman who, on the eve of this country's worst storm, said 'It might be a little windy tomorrow.' Expert or amateur, panglossian or doom-monger, the future can make mugs of us all.

Perhaps there is danger in putting too much store in what might happen tomorrow. As well as betraying the preferences of the predictor, predictions about the future play to the fatalist and the fantasist, and both these outlooks can leave people thinking they can't do anything about the outcomes predicted. We then end up doing nothing and our predictions become self-fulfilling prophesies.

Prophecy and prediction are not the same thing. When the prophets like Jeremiah and Isaiah pointed to terrible events in the future they were not predictions of what would happen, rather descriptions of what could happen if the people didn't change their ways. They were more concerned about getting things right in the present, than being right about the future. They called out uncomfortable truths – sometimes at great personal risk – about the injustices of society, the people's indifference to poverty, or the environment – urging people to change now in order to avoid future catastrophe.

The Jeremiahs maybe long gone, but if we listen carefully, we can still hear the prophets of our day. Not all end up being thrown into a pit or put to death, although of course, some still are. They could be journalists, musicians or even one of your children. They don't need special qualifications. God once used a donkey to prophesy to its hard-hearted owner, and the message doesn't have to be pious, priggish or conventionally religious. The inspiration might be divine, but the action is earthly, urgent and rooted in the now.

Some believe that part of the supernatural outworking of creation is that God has placed the future inside the present. A prophet is someone who is able to describe that future, provoking a change of heart and mind that leads to action. I'd even suggest that anyone who calls out injustice is a prophet, and we are in need of new prophets to speak the truth about what is necessary this year to win a hopeful future for ourselves and the generation to come.

3.1.2019

—

You are what you oat

'Just do it. Because you're worth it. A diamond is forever. It's the real thing. It's the economy stupid. We're going to build a wall. Yes we can!' For good or ill, a slogan or a catchphrase can make the difference between brand recognition or irrelevance, between electoral victory and failure. Slogans can shape our lives.

This was brought home to me while watching *Brexit: The Uncivil War*, a television drama that showed how the Leave campaign won the referendum. In a key scene we see the eureka moment where the campaign director comes up with the slogan 'Take back control'. At last they had a pithy phrase that captured the essence of their message. It's hard to measure how much these three words swung the vote, but they made for a simple and effective slogan.

Complex thinking is in some ways the enemy of the sloganeer. I learnt this as an advertising copywriter where we were usually looking for a line that captured the idea of something as a feeling rather than a rational thought. It was a bonus if it was funny, but that didn't necessarily make it better. As I discovered when my line for a famous brand of porridge, 'You are what you oat', was rejected in favour of 'Buy one get one free.'

The word slogan comes from the Scottish Gaelic meaning 'war cry.' This feels apt at a time when the armies that shout loudest seem to be winning the war of words. For a slogan to work it doesn't have to be positive. Indeed, we're living at a time when negative messages seem more likely to succeed; it's less 'Yes we can' more 'No you won't!' Just say whatever you like, as often as you can, and people will believe it. President Trump's wall offers a curious metaphor for this; whether it happens or not, in some people's minds it's already been built.

To quote a slogan from a real war, 'Careless words cost lives.' The pen may be mightier than the sword but it can be just as destructive if the words written incite fear, hate, prejudice and even war itself. Even a slogan-savvy nation like ours has to be careful to look for the hand that holds the pen, the author behind the words. Your country needs you! Yes, but for what, and who is really asking?

Jesus could play copywriter: 'Do not worry; love your enemies; beware of false prophets', but for me these slogans only mean something because he is their author. Their authority comes from him. He is the embodiment of his words. He doesn't just declaim them he lives and dies by them. The messenger is the message and the medium, the signpost and the slogan, and in these noisy, clanging times we should be wary of believing in any message unless we can also believe its messenger.

10.1.2019

—

United Kingdoms

On Saturday I took the train to Cardiff, a ticket to the rugby match between Wales and Ireland burning in my breast pocket. The carriage was divided evenly between green and red and I found myself sat next to a man from Dublin. We discussed our respective nations' chances and were unified in our hope that, should we fail, the Scots do us an unlikely favour and beat the English. Our conversation moved on to the serious questions facing our United and divided Kingdoms, questions of borders and politics; he reminded me that the Irish rugby team represented two nations not one.

In the stadium the people from our nations gathered to yell and sing their support, to forget and settle differences in sporting combat. Just before kick-off, as the teams, both coached by New Zealanders, lined up, the 70,000 in the stadium kept a minute's silence for the men, women and children killed in Christchurch. We all stood, united against the deeper divisions at play in the world.

When the match started, the heavens opened and rain poured down through the roof which, according to local wisdom, had been left open so that God could watch. Wales scored early and Welsh nerves – like Welsh rain, an especially bubbly brew – were quickly settled. The soaked pilgrims started singing their hymns and arias, and for an hour or two we had enough heavenly bread to feed us till we wanted no more.

At half time the Welsh were happy and the Irish graciously accepting the inevitable. In the gents someone piped up 'There's no back stop in here, boys' and the two tribes were united by laughter. Wales went on to win a Grand Slam – a sort of Holy Grail in rugby although not as rare (if you're Welsh). The Irish, never knowingly out partied, joined in the celebrations by singing along to 'Land Of My Fathers'. In the euphoric giddiness of it all the thought came that this spirit could unite the world.

I knew this spiritedness would pass, but the feeling lasted all the way home where I was happy to accept the congratulations of my English friends and neighbours. In the end, we all must return to our places, our kingdoms. It's only sport, but the events of the day were a reminder that in this United Kingdom we have long had the capacity to hold in tension a fierce tribalism with a mutual regard. The bond expressed in games like these is stronger than the divisions of frontier, class or party that currently weigh so heavily upon us.

Scripture talks about a Kingdom that contains no walls, no divisions, no winners or losers. It calls people in to a unity, and we sometimes glimpse it when people share their lives and see through and beyond their supposed differences. A wet but glorious day in Cardiff reminded me that this other Kingdom is, perhaps, nearer than we think.

19.3.2019

—

Speed awareness

Last week I drove to a business hotel just off the M40. There, I made my way to a room where around 50 people were gathering, each with the same, 'I really don't want to be here' expression on their faces. It was as broad a cross-section of society as you could find. Yet the thing that united us was our common offence; we had all broken the speed limit and were taking the inconvenience of four hours of correction instead of the punishment of points.

Last year, just over a million drivers opted to complete a Speed Awareness Course, as an alternative to receiving fixed penalty points and a fine. The course is designed to change the behaviour of speeding motorists and prevent them from reoffending. Not since school detention had I been in a room full of so many wrong-doers and, just like a detention, we had two choices: moan and get punished again, or use the time to learn something.

At first the mood was recalcitrant. I think many had the feeling that if others deserved to be here, they didn't. We were, to quote the gospel, 'Confident of our own righteousness – and looking down on everyone else.' The entitlement and self-justification in the room was palpable. When asked to confess our offences nearly all offered an excuse: 'I was doing 57 in a 50 but I didn't see the sign,' or 'It didn't feel like 60,' or 'Everyone else was going 75.'

It was like a scene from an existential comedy. With everyone (as Beckett put it), 'Blaming on his boots the fault of his feet.' Thankfully the people running the course knew how to get the best from the players. Instead of compounding our guilt, they asked us why we thought we had broken the speed limit. Then, what the consequences could be for us and others. They showed us how speeding made it worse for everyone. Slowly, through a curious combination of confession and information, the room moved from self-justification and resistance to self-awareness and acceptance.

Someone who's done the course is 23 per cent less likely to speed again than someone who took the points, so there's something in the confession-information formulae. To repent means to change direction and turn around, but it's much easier to turn around when you are given the space to admit you need to, have an understanding of why you need to, and are shown that there's a better way.

As I drove home afterwards, the needle of the speedometer nudging the speed limit, I eased off the accelerator. It was still easy to transgress in this world, but at least I knew I was doing something wrong and had an informed desire not to do so again. When we're heading the wrong way, too fast, awareness that we're doing it is the first step to changing direction and driving to a safer future.

26.3.2019

—

Soul hacker

As one of the one and a half billion users of the WhatsApp messaging system, it was unnerving to learn that hackers had exploited a flaw in the application's security, and installed spyware which can turn a mobile phone into a surveillance system by activating its camera and microphone, tracking your movements, and seeing every message you write.

In the hands of an authoritarian regime this becomes a serious tool of oppression. Although I did wonder what my hacked phone would reveal about my life. Group chats about which pub to watch the football at, an oversharing of opinions on things political, literary and musical. Whether John Snow deserved to be king in *Game of Thrones*. All in all. You'd know nothing.

Yet the incident is a salutary reminder of how much of our privacy we entrust to those who may not have our best interests within their purview, and how careful we should be about what we share of ourselves online. Years ago, when the dangers of the new technology were not obvious, a friend who worked in tech advised me never to send a message that I wasn't prepared for the whole world to see because, sure enough, the world would be able to see it.

Technology has created a double bind. It facilitates communication to an amazing degree. We can send a message to anyone, anywhere, anytime, yet it seems to be coming with an increase in surveillance that makes private communication risky. What to do? Leave that chat group? Throw away the phone and return to writing letters? Or do we become like footballers on the telly, speaking to each other with hands cupping our mouths for fear that others might we see what we're saying?

In a famous psalm an exhausted and oppressed David half-complains, half-rejoices in the truth that he is unable to escape the omniscient God he believes in. 'Where can I hide from your spirit?' he asks. He answers his own question by saying that he can't and that perhaps it doesn't matter. He knows that God's gaze not only penetrates the rock of the cave in which he hides, it sees into his very soul. God is able to read his life, decrypt it end-to-end.

The idea of being soul-hacked would be appalling if the one doing the hacking was a malignant force out to mine the data of our lives and use the information for their own ends to crush and oppress us. Yet as the Psalmist goes on to say, 'Your eyes have seen my unformed substance. Created my inmost being.'

He's telling us we have nothing to fear. The One who cracks the encryption of our hearts, created the heart *and* gives us the code to open it. The One who is watching us, in this instance, is not against us but for us.

17.5.2019

—

Amazing Grace

Amazing Grace, a documentary about the recording of Aretha Franklin's gospel album in a Baptist church in 1972, is a rare example of something that lives up to even the most hyperbolic praise. I saw it in my local cinema last week and it is, I think, amazing, although I can't fully explain what it is that makes it so.

Perhaps you had to be there. The film-makers certainly make you feel you are there, in this badly lit, poorly ventilated church with its cheap seats and tacky mural. There is, of course, that voice, voted by

Rolling Stone magazine as the greatest of the twentieth century. Then there's Aretha's dignified presence at the pulpit, the hum of her celebrity low in the mix as she gets down to the serious business of praising the God she believes in. The background noise of her troubled upbringing only adds to the authenticity. When she sings the title track, we believe her; she isn't so much performing as testifying.

It was like being invited to a religious experience, and it seemed that some in the cinema were having one. Half way through the film I realised the man next to me was weeping, shaking his head and saying 'It's too much. It's too much.' When Aretha's pianist, the Reverend James Cleveland, asks: 'Can I get a witness?' a number of people in the cinema actually yelled out 'Yes!'

So what is this grace and what is so amazing about it? It's a lovely word. How sweet the sound. It bleeds into the language: it's there in gratitude for a gift; for work done gratis, in the grace before a meal, and in the grace notes supplied by a composer. It's rooted in a beautiful concept, that of God's love coming among us, free of charge, no religious hoop-jumping, no proving your worth. It's an invitation that even extends to a wretch like me.

Receiving something we don't deserve is hard. In a world based on merit we expect to earn it. Like the man said, it's too much. I am not worthy. As if aware of this inbuilt resistance to receiving unmerited gifts, Jesus chose to *describe* grace rather than explain it; in parables full of topsy-turvy values, where prodigal children are generously welcomed home, the sun shines on good and bad alike, and the least limp over the line first.

He never used the word, but his own words were so full of grace, their spirit lives on in words and song. The reaction in that cinema suggested to me there is a great hunger for grace, especially now. This echo of a tune we have not heard but recognize when we hear it. It is too much for some people, but that is the point. That is the amazing thing about grace.

24.5.2019

Nationalism versus patriotism

What is the difference between a patriot and a nationalist? Sadly, this isn't a joke, but it is a question worth asking in the light of rising nationalism throughout the world.

Can you be one and not the other? Einstein, Orwell and a few Old Testament prophets certainly thought so. Einstein said nationalism was 'an infantile sickness; the measles of the human race'. Orwell defined nationalism as loyalty to any cause or group, be it creed, race or country, that 'recognized no other duty other than the advancement of its own interests'. He contrasts this with patriotism which represents a devotion to a particular place or way of life but without any feeling of having to force it on others. A patriot might insist they live in the best place in the world, but they have the good humour to recognize the same impulse when someone from, say, Spain makes the same claim. As a boy I sent a letter to my parents. I wrote the address of our house, street, town, county, then added Wales, United Kingdom, Europe, The World, The Solar System, The Universe. Underlining Wales lest the postman wonder where I came from.

Nationalism is different to patriotism. I think the nationalist wants to secure power and prestige for whatever cause or entity they have sunk their individuality into and will often be willing to do whatever it takes to get their way. Where patriotism doesn't need an enemy, nationalism seems to demand one. It is exclusive, not inclusive, and it's especially dangerous when whole countries become nationalistic. Then the actions of a country are no longer judged as good or bad, but by who does them. Mass deportations or the imprisoning of people without trial might start to happen but are justified because *they are* the country doing it.

Rampant nationalism in its various guises (idolatry, indifference to others, violence) is what most of the Old Testament prophets spoke out against. Often at great personal cost. While false prophets flattered the nation by condemning the actions of people in other lands, the likes of Jeremiah and Amos had the gall to point to similar injustices happening in their own back yard. Look, they said, we deceive ourselves if we don't recognize that we are doing the same and worse.

These prophets challenged people to think about where their loyalties lie: was it to family, town or country? To the poor? To God? Or should it belong to all of the above. They called people to right action in the affairs of the heart as well as state. In this way they were true patriots. There is in their words the powerful implication that you can't love your country, without first loving the people you live among and recognizing your connection to the people over there, in the world, the solar system, the universe.

15.8.2019

—

No class

In the last few weeks there has been a noticeable increase in class-laden insults being exchanged between political opponents. A working class minister has been accused of not having enough GCSEs to do her job. Speakers at a Labour conference have talked of posh boys and banning private schools. While those who say we should find some kind of middle ground are told they're out of touch with real people and living in a liberal, elite bubble.

All this has a retrograde feel. Harking back to a time when we were stuck with rigid, fatalistic class distinctions, as so brilliantly captured in the 1962 comedy sketch on the *Frost Report*, where an absurdly tall, upper class John Cleese feels superior to a middle class Ronnie Barker, who in turn looks down on a lower class Ronnie Corbett – who 'knows his place'. Back then there were even finer calibrations of class to worry about. I was born into a middle-class family that had lower-middle class provenance (being 'trade'), but which (through education and occupation) had upper-middle class pretentions and connections. I knew my place, but I soon began to learn that it wasn't as fixed as I thought. At my state primary school, I felt posh; at my direct grant boarding school I felt somewhere in the middle; it wasn't until I went to university that I realized what upper class really looked like. When I fell in love with a working-class girl, a friend actually asked me if it was sensible to go out with someone from a different background.

Years later, when the Berlin Wall came down, some said the class war was over. The proletariat hadn't risen up because they really wanted colour TVs. In this country, we entered what the then Tory Prime Minister, John Major, called The Classless Society. Under Tony Blair's New Labour, the phrase 'social mobility' was coined. You no longer had to 'know your place' because you could move – on and up.

Today many barriers of class have, like the wall, come down; but certain differences – particularly economic ones – are still unresolved. 'The poor you will always have with you' (and the posh, too) remains an inconvenient truth. Thankfully, that working-class girl I met (and later married) was smart and classy enough to introduce me to the source of that particular truth.

When Jesus engaged with people, their social background was rarely the issue. Yes, he subverted ideas of hierarchy and pecking order; we are all equal in the eyes of God, if not the Inland Revenue. His real concern was for the individual's soul. When he met someone – tax collector, fisherman, army officer, prostitute – he addressed their particularity. His gospel inverts the condescension inherent in that sketch, as well as the class-laden insults being thrown around today. In His world people are judged, not by their class or status, but by their attitude to others.

26.9.2019

—

Man in a ditch

In the park near my home there is a man, lying in a ditch, using the sod for a bed and cardboard boxes for a duvet. When it rains he heads to the library to keep dry and read the papers until it closes. If he'd read the papers this week he'd have seen, among headlines about deadlines and red lines, that 726 homeless people died last year. The Office for National Statistics declared it the biggest increase in homeless deaths since such data was first collected.

The causes of these deaths are as varied and complex as the people who lost their lives, but drug use and the loss of a safety net are being cited as key factors. The Housing Minister said 'There is no shying away from these statistics'; his shadow said the findings 'Shamed us all,' while the Chief Executive of Crisis said 'It is heart-breaking that hundreds of people were forced to spend the last days of their lives without the dignity of a secure home.'

Indeed, it is a scandal that, in one of the richest nations on earth, people die in ditches and on street corners for want of shelter, warmth and help. Yet it seems we still inhabit a world where, to quote the prophet, Job, the homeless 'Have nothing to cover themselves in the cold' and 'the cries of the dying rise from the city.'

Of course, there are people responding to these cries. Charitable organizations, care workers, churches, stitching together a patchwork of support as best they can. Where I live a charity gets churches to convert into hostels for the night and its people to cook, serve and eat food with the homeless who come. It's basically people with homes serving people without, which is about the only difference between them.

For these encounters show that behind every statistic there is a story. A person with a name, who once had a home, but whose life went awry. There are many routes to homelessness: a simple twist of fate, a redundancy, a divorce, a bout of depression, a battle with addiction. All of them situations closer to home than those with homes might like to hear. As the gospel suggests, one reason it's uncomfortable getting close to poverty and weakness is that it lays bare our own poverty and weakness.

Meanwhile, the man in the park has moved on. He has his own potentially lethal deadline to worry about. The weather is changing. You can feel the presage of colder days in the air as the mercury drops below 10 degrees. For most of us this means pulling on a jumper or popping the heating on; for him and the thousands who walk the streets without the succour of shelter, it signals the approach of more challenging questions: Will I get through this winter? And what help will I find?

03.10.2019

—

Interventionist God

The devastating news that the bodies of 39 people were found in the back of a container in Essex yesterday, shocks and breaks hearts, demands and confounds explanation. For those poor people, it seems our sadness and outrage has come too late. Only awful questions remain. How could this happen? Did anyone hear their cries? Why did no one intervene? My God, why have you forsaken them?

The musician Nick Cave has a song that opens with the lament 'I don't believe in an interventionist God.' And I confess that events like these make faith in a God who intervenes hard to hold on to. Cave himself went on to experience great loss when his teenage son died. He has released two deeply moving albums since that tragedy, both lyrically haunted by his grief and raising questions about where his faith is in the face of suffering. 'Sometimes,' he sings, 'it's better not to say anything – at all.' Terrible events leave us mute. The words run out.

Yet still, prayers and thoughts and feelings go out (some to an interventionist God, some not). Even though they sometimes seem to come back void, unanswered or unheard, we send them out.

Sometimes in the face of impossible odds. Like the prayers for my friend who, following heart surgery, lies vulnerable in his hospital bed, his life in the balance. I know he wants me to pray, because he has asked me to, so I do. As an act of solidarity and love, if not faith. Even though with every prayer the questions flash back – why bother? Is anybody out there? What difference will it make? I do it anyway.

What if you do believe in an interventionist God? The whole crux of faith in Christ hangs on this. The hope in a God who has, does and will intervene. Not an indifferent, deist God spectating from afar – but one who is involved, who is present. Even then, suffering awakes doubts about the nearness – the existence – of such a God. Jesus, who, some believe, embodies the promise of God's intervention in our world, put no theory forward about suffering. He made no conjectures. He did not enter into the tricky arguments about cause and effect and blame in which people tried to draw him. Faced with suffering he was just deeply moved by it. His compassion was the answer given to the question.

If, with the news of the deaths of the 39 people, we are left with only sadness and outrage, that is something. For if we are angry, we are not indifferent. If we are moved, we are involved. We are giving our voice to the 39 whose lives have been so cruelly silenced. These responses may well be part of what prayer is, and they contain the possibility that we are part of the answer.

24.10.2019

—